How to Get
a Museum Job

How to Get a Museum Job

Steven Miller

ROWMAN & LITTLEFIELD
Lanham • Boulder • New York • London

Published by Rowman & Littlefield
A wholly owned subsidiary of The Rowman & Littlefield Publishing Group, Inc.
4501 Forbes Boulevard, Suite 200, Lanham, Maryland 20706
www.rowman.com

6 Tinworth Street, London SE11 5AL, United Kingdom

British Library Cataloguing in Publication Information Available

Library of Congress Cataloging-in-Publication Data

Names: Miller, Steven, 1947– author.
Title: How to get a museum job / Steven Miller.
Description: Lanham, MD : Rowman & Littlefield, [2019] | Includes
    bibliographical references and index.
Identifiers: LCCN 2018054399 (print) | LCCN 2018055891 (ebook) | ISBN
    9781538121115 (Electronic) | ISBN 9781538121092 (cloth : alk. paper) |
    ISBN 9781538121108 (pbk. : alk. paper)
Subjects: LCSH: Museums—Vocational guidance—United States. | Museums
    —United States—Employees.
Classification: LCC AM11 (ebook) | LCC AM11 .M64 2019 (print) | DDC
    069.023—dc23
LC record available at https://lccn.loc.gov/2018054399

♾️™ The paper used in this publication meets the minimum requirements of
American National Standard for Information Sciences—Permanence of Paper
for Printed Library Materials, ANSI/NISO Z39.48-1992.

Printed in the United States of America

While museums are about the present and the past, this book
is about the future. It is dedicated to the next generation
of museum workers. I know you will move the field forward
in exciting ways and respect the legacies entrusted to you!

Contents

List of Illustrations

Preface

This is an exciting time for museums. They are popular centers of trusted and readily accessed knowledge about the human and natural universe. Few communities do not boast at least one. Most have several. Cities have many. New museums are being created with astonishing frequency for all sorts of subjects and for all sorts of reasons. Existing museums expand with almost predetermined regularity.

How to Get a Museum Job is designed to help aspiring museum workers successfully compete for full-time employment in today's museum renaissance. The book is written especially for entry-level professionals or those still in the early stages of their careers. The advice offered will also be of service to individuals well along on their employment paths. And, it will be of value for those wishing to make lateral moves into the museum field from other fields. This is a growing phenomenon that is welcome and will continue.

The increase in and expansion of museums around the globe is resulting in a host of positions to be filled by qualified candidates. This employment buildup has also seen a reinvigorated emphasis on reconfiguring or strengthening existing jobs.

In concert with the rise of museums has been a welcome and long overdue advancement in the professionalization of their operations. The improvement is especially apparent in the personnel arena. These unique institutions are no longer quiet enclaves for people with well-meaning if amateur interests in the sciences, arts, and history. Employees are now specifically trained and expected to perform at a high level of accomplishment in various disciplines.

There is no book exclusively tailored to finding work in museums, as written from inside the field. Recognizing this absence, *How to Get a Museum Job* is structured to be as practical as possible for job hunters. Some personal philosophy and opinion is expressed, but only if it amplifies or supports an employment point. The idea is to understand customary hiring paths in this diverse field while providing an overall introduction to standard museum positions.

Museums require an atypical blend of employees. Because of the unusual civic role these institutions embrace, staffing calls for a diverse mix of talents, abilities, interests, and skills. Any list of positions is telling. There are assignments for everyone. Though the competition may seem daunting, well-prepared, qualified, pragmatic applicants are usually successful in finding jobs they want and like.

Museum operations rely on a diverse range of talents, personalities, interests, and academic backgrounds. We encounter scientists, bookkeepers, teachers, sales associates, historians, artists, mechanics, fundraisers, and guards, to name a few. All have to work together in a productive and collegial manner to meet a lofty mission while contributing individual content benefits. The diverse personnel mix operates under the auspices of a governing body that usually has no experience in any of the employee areas of responsibility. That body is usually known as a board of trustees.

And, speaking of trustees, this book is also written with them in mind. Given their role as fiduciaries securing the well-being of the nonprofit sector of America, they are responsible for valued endeavors that exist for public good. Because staffing is so important to the success of any entity, trustees must be aware of how museum people should be sought, treated, and hired. Usually they are not directly involved in specific employment decisions, but an understanding of the process is important. An exception to their absence of hiring involvement is for the director of a museum. These positions are almost always filled through board searches.

The saying that an organization's most important asset is its staff applies to museums, to a degree. Actually there is a complex mix to assets. These must be understood by job applicants and are discussed in more detail in the chapter on interviewing.

Essentially museums are amalgams of disparate and sometimes peculiar assets. In no priority order these include the following attributes:

- Reason for Existing

    It is not entirely facetious to say there is a museum for every subject imaginable. Sometimes these reasons can be assets while at other times they might be deficits. When looking for work you need to decide if the subject of a particular museum suits you. You will be a more convincing job applicant when you want to work at a museum that has a mission you believe in. Both your interest and the museum's purpose will be melded assets.

- Collections

  Museums are known by their collections. Great museums have great collections. Weak museums either have few or obscure collections. Think about what you will be working with or around. Do you like these things? Do they make sense to have? Can you explain why they are important? Since most museum collections are not on view most of the time, are you comfortable with that and can you explain it in a satisfactory manner if need be?

- Facilities

  Museums carry out their work in all sorts of buildings and with all sorts of facilities. These can be both assets and challenges. Look closely at structures and equipment when seeking work.

- Programs

  Museum programming can be a tremendous asset. When applying for a particular job, look closely at what is done already, and think about what can be done, especially by you, if a job entails programming. (Maintenance, security, and finance positions usually have little to do with initiating programming but a lot to do with helping make it a success.)

- Location

  Where a museum is located can be an asset. Those that are hard to get to, are open infrequently, or have a low public profile are usually less attractive places to work. This is true be they in urban, suburban, or rural sites. Think about location when looking at a job. Avoid applying to any that are where you prefer not to be.

- Finances

  Financial stability is an obvious museum asset for many reasons. It is especially important for employees. Be careful when considering a particular museum for a job. How does its balance sheet read? What has been its finance history? Working for a museum with an annual balanced budget, no matter how small, is to be preferred over working for one that may get a lot of attention but is a fiscally failing museum. This predicament is no secret to the public, donors, and staff, and can make an employee's work difficult.

- Longevity

  Museum longevity can be an asset as it suggests stability, accomplishment, and acceptance by a public, or at least a core of supporters over the years. Periodically though, museums of long-standing can experience downturns. Job applicants are advised to assess the operating health of museums that have been around a long time.

- Staff

  Most museum staff are a delight to work with and are indeed an institutional asset. There will, of course, be strengths and weaknesses, and job

applicants are advised to learn about employees, especially those they will
work closely with.

- Governing Authority

    All American museums have some sort of governing authority to watch
    over them. For government-owned and -operated museums, this will be
    a town, county, state or national department, office, agency, or agencies.
    Because most museums in the United States are private, they are governed
    by a board of trustees. This body does not own the museum or any part of
    it but serves on behalf of the general public to steward the organization.
    Legal oversight is usually provided by a state's attorney general. When
    looking at a museum job, try to assess the trustees to determine if they
    are a valued asset. Museums owned by other entities such as colleges or
    universities will not have their own board with the same legal authority as
    a private, stand-alone museum.

- Volunteers

    Museums rely on volunteers to support many aspects of their opera-
    tions. Excellent volunteers are a treasured asset. Occasionally that is not
    the case. Job applicants are encouraged to inquire about a museum's vol-
    unteer circumstances.

    On a day-to-day basis, museums are group efforts. The group can be
    large or small and made up of salaried, hourly, seasonal, as well as volun-
    teer participants. As in life, some individuals will be introverted and oth-
    ers extroverted. Often they are in jobs ideally suited to these personality
    profiles. Registrars may avoid being outgoing while marketing staff will
    do the opposite.

The component pieces that make up museums may evolve from staff im-
pacts, but the needs are fluid and not readily ascribed to specific individuals
all the time. Complications play out daily on the job. Deciphering an employment atmosphere is critical for job seekers. It is tough to do during a
hiring process but well worth trying. Appearances can be deceiving. Given
the scope of personalities encountered in museums, it can take time to learn
what everyone is really like and how well they get along. Actually, given the
different assignments personnel have, they often coexist without conflicts because there are no overlapping responsibilities and few want to do another's
job or know what it is anyway.

How people interact at work can make or break an organization or aspects
of it. Again, this is true of all undertakings be they in government, the business world, or the nonprofit sector. It is a fact that makes wise and effective
hiring a management first priority. Increasingly interviewers probe candidates' abilities and willingness to work collegially with coworkers, the pub-

lic, and other museum interests on the job. Aspiring museum workers need to do the same of prospective museum employers.

Deciding and agreeing upon who does what, how, and why, within museums, has resulted in an overall list of assignments enumerated in specific job titles and descriptions. Policy statements, governing documents, and institutional printed matter may suggest employment security. On the job things can be quite different. Given the rise of museums as civic powerhouses, there is more staff movement within the field than ever. Consequently, job opportunities are frequent. They may perhaps not be always what one wants at a given time or where one would prefer to work, but the options nevertheless remain promising.

How to Get a Museum Job concentrates on full-time employment. Certainly temporary or contract arrangements are fine, but most of us want something longer lasting (and with benefits!). To be sure, our lives may sometimes call for part-time positions. This might be especially true for new parents, students, or others for whom a forty-hour week is impractical, unnecessary, or unavailable. The last circumstance may call for taking any sort of advantageous position that helps one gain experience and improve the résumé while a permanent job remains to be found.

Some of what is contained here is obvious. Readers will be apt to say, "Any fool knows to show up to an interview on time." However, I am amazed at how often the most customary aspects of job hunting are forgotten by the hunters or the hunted. Indeed, I have committed a faux pas or two, myself. One would think common sense alone would keep mistakes absent. But, as my late mother would say, "Common sense is no common thing." Right on, Ann Miller!

ORGANIZATION

Chapter 1 puts museums in a historical context and discusses their current characteristics. Their origins continue to define them, especially when new ones are created. The ways museums prove their worth is in flux, but their core reasons for existing rarely change. Outside forces are influencing museums more than ever. Pressures are expressed by political, economic, scholarly, and social interests. Museum employees need to be aware of and prepared for influences of diverse origins.

The chapter touches on how well an individual must know him- or herself to pursue a rewarding museum career. On the job, a common understanding of the institution you work in is absolutely necessary. Usually this is declared in a formal mission statement. On the job, how that unfolds can vary. When applying for a particular museum job, assess how the definition of that museum is expressed and shared by staff you encounter during interviews or in outside conversations.

Chapter 2 lists the primary jobs found in the museum field. A brief description of each is included along with what academic credentials are required and the sorts of personalities that gravitate to particular jobs. From positions that call for no or little post-high school classroom time, to positions that reflect very high levels of study, the variety of jobs in museums is wide to say the least. Because of the exceptional nature of museum directing, comments on this position are longer than for other museum posts.

Museums are quizzically philosophical undertakings. They have no practical reason to exist, hence their reliance on emotional connectivity. The feelings upon which museums are based need to be understood internally and externally by all personnel. *How to Get a Museum Job* places its advisory emphasis on what those with jobs and those seeking jobs believe is important for the employees of a particular museum. For whatever reason, this is not discussed by practitioners at length in any other publication about museum work.

Given the incredible variety of museums, chapter 3 examines and synthesizes their diverse range and nature for people to consider when seeking employment. Small, large, new, old, rich, poor, urban, rural—you name it—and a museum can be found with those and many, many other characteristics. One size does not fit all, and prospective employees need to think hard about what will suit them. If an initial job decision proves unsatisfactory, it is relatively easy to move on in the museum field provided your résumé is unblemished and your work experience logical and impressive. This is true even for those who encounter difficulties that might otherwise scuttle a career.

Having defined and described museums and museum positions, chapter 4 outlines the process of finding museum work. Today there are a host of sites listing positions. I have always found job announcements to be of great value in assessing the state of museum work generally. An occasional cursory review, even when not seeking employment, can provide insights into where the field is and where it might be headed. Of course, personal contacts within the field, schmoozing, and luck all play important roles when job hunting. Relying on job ads alone narrows your options.

Chapter 5 discusses application processes. Obtaining official policies and other documents will be extremely advantageous during a search. The more research a candidate does about a museum the better. This can be accomplished online, with visits to a prospective employer, and through conversations with colleagues. Museums are pretty transparent in many respects. Prior to applying for a job, the more a candidate knows about a prospective employer the better. This knowledge will also hold one in good stead during an interview.

Given the communications that unfold if successful job application contact is made with a museum employer, chapters 6 and 7 delve into the intricacies of a job interview. This encounter can make or break a candidate's chances of success. Preparing to respond to and ask the questions noted will give candidates an advantage. Please think of more. Chapter 6 lists questions museums will ask applicants. Chapter 7 lists questions applicants can ask museums. An ideal interview is a two-way street.

Chapter 8 discusses museum job search variables. It includes notes about working with search firms. It discusses lateral moves for people thinking about changing careers. And, it includes a short note about the demographics of museum hiring.

Chapter 9 contains an overview of the future of museum jobs. While museums may seem stable and even static, they are subject to forces causing a range of changes. These forces are caused internally as well as externally. Most museum jobs will remain in place, but the scope and content of their work will alter according to variable pressures from the museum field itself and outside influences. Positions that might have been assigned mostly scholarly duties might increasingly be assigned public visitor engagement work.

Few people are blessed to make a living at a lifelong passion. I am one of those. Since joyously accepting my first full-time museum job in 1971, I have never regretted my career choice. This is an exciting time for museums. On a local, national, or international level, I believe it is a golden age for these unique institutions. The present is impressive, and the future is bright. In concert with the rise of museums as forums for cultural identities has come a welcome, indeed long overdue, increase and improvement in their professional levels of operation. Consequentially, staffing museums is now a far more rigorous and serious concern than it has ever been. Amateurs and those obviously unqualified for certain jobs are usually denied consideration when positions are being filled. Today, much is required of a prospective employer and a prospective employee when it comes to both creating and getting positions. Alterations in how museums see themselves have had a significant impact on museum jobs. Museum work encompasses a wide range of specialties. Each requires specific training. This book reflects one perspective on the current state of museum employment realities. It is written "from the inside" by someone with many years of service in these wonderful and still novel places. I wish you good fortune as you pursue work in one of the most unusual areas of employment imaginable.

Chapter One

The Museum and You

Potential museum employees should have an understanding of the current museum scene. This is not difficult to do. Immerse yourself in museum professional organizations, go to their meetings, read their publications, and study whatever books online or in hard copy that are relevant to your interests. There is an excellent museum studies "library" available these days, and it covers the full gamut of occupations, from conservation to visitor services, from security to retail sales, from education to collection management, from maintenance to media.

Museums are found all over. More and more are started every year. They seem to regularly grow. Museums are owned by governments, academic institutions, companies, individuals, and groups. Their effectiveness and impact can vary dramatically according to size, governance, operational capabilities, where they are, what subject(s) they focus on, and their financial stability.

A BRIEF HISTORY OF MUSEUMS

Without delving into a lengthy history of the origins of museums, a brief overview will be helpful for those looking for work in them. Museums as we know them are a product of the Enlightenment and the Age of Exploration. They are European inventions with roots that trace to private collections, art and relics found in houses of worship, and the décor of places of public assembly. In those settings, people would encounter the sorts of objects cherished by the wealthy, loved by clergy, or used for civic promotions in government settings. Sculpture, paintings, and fancy decorations, as well as natural history specimens and curios from around the globe were once seen only in private homes, churches, government centers, etc. Now they are also seen in museums.

In time, the intellectual, emotional, and financial value of objects of all sorts led people to think about keeping them together in some public place for the greater public good. This concept included the notion of long-term retention. On the surface, the notion may be considered unrealistic, but in practice, it is an operating principal for every museum.

The common manifestation of the museum unfolded in the eighteenth century. A few prominent institutions still operating include the Louvre (1793) in Paris, France; the Kuntskamera (1727) in St. Petersburg, Russia; the Charlestown Museum (1773) in Charleston, South Carolina; the Rijksmuseum (1800) in Amsterdam, Netherlands; and the British Museum (1753) in London, Great Britain.

The nineteenth century saw the creation of thousands of museums across Europe and in hemispheres touched by the European Diaspora. They were formed for various reasons. They were mechanisms for academic pursuits, machines for political propaganda, and ways to celebrate noteworthy individuals, events, peoples, and places. This continues to the present.

As museums became reality, two distinct operating structures emerged reflecting two distinct political approaches to providing public service. In most countries around the globe, museums are owned by governments. While there are government-owned museums in the United States, most are privately owned and managed by a board of trustees as nonprofit, tax-exempt entities.

THE MUSEUM WORLD

How to Get a Museum Job encompasses advice given to me and advice I have given to others about looking for museum work. It reflects the varying employment contexts of a unique career field. That arena is getting more complex. There are several reasons for this. Since the 1960s in particular, museums have elevated their professional game. The qualitative results are apparent in all operating areas, be it behind the scenes or in direct view of the public. More overt and obvious institutional purposes have seen a meteoric increase in people's admiration for museums as valuable civic endeavors. Museums have caused the public to have high expectations when it comes to exhibits, programs, scholarship, social engagement, and inclusive cultural respect. Consequently, employees must meet increasingly high levels of accomplishment in their chosen area of work.

For the purposes of job hunting, I define museums as:

A public service preservation organization that explains subjects through objects, and those objects are generally original to a museum's mission from a historical, artistic, or scientific perspective.

Please note that while an institution defines itself as a museum, the word *museum* may not be in an organization's title. A museum can be known as a gallery, collection, center, historical society, etc. A few examples would be the Frick Collection or the Brooklyn Historical Society, both in New York City; the National Gallery of Art in Washington, DC; or the Franklin Institute in Philadelphia, PA. There is no legal requirement for any museum to use the word *museum* in its name.

A host of businesses share aspects of what museums do. These include commercial art galleries, antiques shops, rock and mineral stores, and auction houses. Some of the advice provided in this book will help when applying for jobs in these sectors. For example, collection managers are used by auction houses to catalogue merchandise. Curatorial skills are critical to catalogue writing and selling in galleries. Conservation is critical to the care of objects for sale. Visitor services skills work well on any "selling floor." Exhibition preparators are used to pack, ship, and display things for sale.

As recognized mainstream economic, social, education, or cultural entities, museums enjoy lofty cerebral and emotional attention, whether deserved or not. Their astonishing rise in public recognition and civic positioning in recent years has seen a vast increase in the number and kinds of jobs within the museum universe. Museums are hot.

The majority of museums (at least ones you would want to work in) are formally structured when it comes to how they are run. Every museum has an organization chart of positions and how they fit into functioning hierarchies. There are usually official job descriptions. Reporting mechanisms and expectations are in place. Personnel policies and manuals exist. Museums not only have mission statements but strategic plans. Boards of trustees have bylaws. There are committees of all sorts, and the duties of each are documented. There is a regular schedule of governance and staff meetings. Museums are more accountable (or should be!) to their audiences, governing oversight agencies, and the general populace. Potential employees of a museum are advised to obtain as much of this information as possible prior to applying for a job. A list of items is provided in chapter 3.

YOU AND A MUSEUM LIFE

The seventeenth-century French philosopher René Descartes curtly summarized human nature with his observation *cogito ergo sum,* "I think therefore I am." That intellectual truism needs to be put into practice every day to prove our worth. It is especially important to apply in pursuing one's livelihood. However, it cannot be fully embraced without also accepting the earlier Greek Delphic aphorism to "know thyself." People seeking museum jobs must have a good sense about why they have selected this line of work.

With certain exceptions, most museum jobs call for some passion about the raison d'être of a particular institution and the broader group that it is part of. No museum wants to hire indifferent employees. Few of us want to work with such people. When looking at jobs, try to assess the emotional commitment to the particular museum by those associated with it, and how committed you will be. By "associated" I mean staff, volunteers, contract services, and especially the board of trustees.

How to Get a Museum Job references the standard positions one is likely to find and seek in the field. The variety of employment specialties is wide. There is something for everyone regardless of professional aspiration or personality. Some museum jobs are specific to these unique institutions, while others are found elsewhere also. The former would include curators, conservators, and exhibition designers, while the latter would include accountants, maintenance, and security staff. Museum work is no different from other lines of work when it comes to expecting certain employees to have certain academic qualifications. Entry level staff doing more than maintenance or security duties will usually pursue graduate studies in relevant fields of interest or in overall museum studies generally.

When contemplating a job in the museum field, it is essential to understand what these places are, why they exist, and how they accomplish what they do. Getting more detailed information about the museum field is not difficult. The American Alliance of Museums (AAM, http://www.aam-us .org) is an excellent place to start. Its website is full of valued information regarding aspects of museum work. The American Association for State and Local History (AASLH, http://www.aaslh.org) is equally helpful. Each has been in existence a long time. They have been singularly instrumental in setting and raising the standards of American museums in particular. Both have employment links on their websites. They have magazines, online newsletters, and other communiqués that should be read. They organize annual meetings as well as workshops and other learning opportunities. In addition, there are regional and state museum membership organizations well worth joining. In fact, these can often provide more personal connectivity to the museum universe.

The fine reputation museums currently enjoy means they are subject to more scrutiny than ever before. This attention is manifested in heightened publicity (positive or otherwise) in hard copy or in online press and social media. Employees now need to accept the fact that they work in glass houses (sometimes literally as museum architects seem to love glass walls and lots of them). Anything that happens in a museum can be the subject of public conversation.

As a job seeker, finding satisfying work in any profession is an obvious positive goal. As an employer, finding good workers is critical to an operation's success and beneficial continuity, not to mention bottom line. This book is written primarily for job seekers. Museum officials and especially those responsible for human relations (aka, HR) are welcome to glean whatever they wish from *How to Get a Museum Job*.

In deciding why one wants to work in a museum and what job would be appropriate, it is important to eliminate positions of no interest. Being a finance person has never held any appeal for me, and I have thus avoided that work. Education has not been at the top of my list nor has maintenance and security. Because I love museum collections, curating was always a top desire. Directing came in second. Though I have directed three museums, I approached the job as a higher form of curating. Sometimes this made sense. Sometimes the idea was wishful thinking.

When considering a museum job, talk to people who have them. There is nothing like meeting with practitioners to learn about what they do and why. Many museum employees are more than willing to help aspiring entry-level folks with career advice. I had the incredible luck to meet with the director of the Metropolitan Museum of Art when I was first looking for a job. He then turned me over to his distinguished assistant director. Both conversations were fairly one-way as I had little to contribute other than my enthusiasm for museum work. These men were generous and gracious and enormously helpful. I recall them with gratitude to this day.

I cite my early enthusiasm for museum work because that is essential when seeking a job in the field. As an employer, I have no interest in hiring someone who is ambivalent about a position. I want people who are committed to the higher altruistic ideals of museums. There is a reason they are philanthropies and fall into the nonprofit charitable tax sector.

Employees must accept and embrace the public service aspect of their jobs in the context of the larger operation and the field in general. This might be a tall order, but in my experience, I have found the best staff understand and are proud of where they work and why. This has always included those who are responsible for non-museum-specific jobs. Being involved in the maintenance of a commercial building will require similar skills as those for the maintenance of a museum, but the purposes are quite different. Providing security for an auto dealership is of value, but protecting fine art, important historic artifacts, and rare natural history specimens has more meaning. Assuring careful, accurate, and honest accounting for a treasured cultural institution is closer to the heart than doing so for some heartless corporation.

And then there is the matter of money to consider when seeking a museum job. Most museum positions do not pay very much. In the distant past, this was often of minimal concern. In those times, leadership positions such as directing and curating were often filled by people with independent personal financial means. They came from private wealth, married into private wealth, or were supported by spouses with ample income. As expectations for museum staffing have altered, pay scales are under severe scrutiny by job applicants and current employees. There is a robust conversation in the field to change compensation. A revealing survey was conducted in 2017 titled "Leaving the Museum Field." The four freelance participants who organized the project found that the main reason people left museum work was because of low salaries.[1] The AASLH will soon take only job ads that list pay ranges. Would that other groups do the same.

Very few people know how museums operate. This includes trustees and others in positions of authority. When contemplating a career in this field, it is important to know that part of your job will be explaining it to others. These may be colleagues, friends, family, donors, funders, politicians, the media, and the public. Explaining projects, procedures, skills, etc. can be enjoyable as it allows employees the opportunity to promote both "their" museum and the work they do.

When applying for a museum job, keep in mind what *your* professional education opportunities might be. Museums are great places for personal learning. Assess how your knowledge will benefit once you are on a job. Self-learning can grow from any museum position, be it curation, maintenance, security, public relations, conservation, collections management, education, visitor services, etc.

Recognizing that museums excel at learning whether for the general public or personally, pay careful attention to those you will be working with. This attention must especially center on the person or persons you will report to. Try to understand their personalities, capabilities, and interests. Investigate the academic credentials of the museum's staff as well as their verifiable experience. After all, you will be similarly examined as a candidate. A maintenance employee may not have a PhD but be superb as a plumber, electrician, carpenter, or mechanic. Public relations staff should have a recognized record of positive promotional successes for the museum. Ask these folks about their contacts. Do they include the customary media outlets museums strive to be seen in?

Some of the smartest, most interesting people I have met in life have been colleagues in the museum field, on the job or off. Most directors are. Exhibit designers can convey creative ways of visually thinking. Curators should be sources of exceptional knowledge, especially if they have been in a particular position for some years. What they know is impressive to say the least. It is not easily contained in books, online, in files, or documented in catalogue records. Whatever position you seek at a museum, presumably there will be employees of substance to learn from. If you are one of them, please continue to share what you learn.

CONCLUSION

At their core, museums are places of celebration, exploration, reassurance, escape, discovery, fascination, and respite. It is hard to think of a subject, place, event, idea, or people not discussed in or by a museum. On a local, national, and international level, a golden age of museums has dawned. With this has come a flowering of job opportunities. *Getting a Museum Job* is designed to help those of us who love these unique institutions, succeed in, and with them. The more you know about the American museum world, the more comfortable you will be in assessing and deciding your preferred place in it.

NOTE

1. Sarah Erdman, Claudia Ocello, Dawn Estabrook Salerno, and Marieke Van Damme, "Leaving the Museum Field," *Alliance Blog*, September 22, 2017, https://www.aam-us.org/2017/09/22/leaving-the-museum-field/.

Chapter Two

Types of Museum Jobs

The museum field has various specific professional disciplines and jobs within it. These require specialized training, be it academic or manual in nature (or a little of both). It is common for people to select employment tracks early in their careers now. There is less fluidity or crossing over between or among job interests. Educators are educators, curators are curators, conservators are conservators, exhibition designers are exhibition designers, etc. Each could land jobs as directors in time, but usually people with such administrative tendencies will start small and work their way up over time.

> In looking for museum work, apply only for a position appropriate for your abilities, experience, and interests; otherwise you're wasting everyone's time and you'll be sorely disappointed.

The following list describes customary museum job categories, in no order of priority or emphasis. The list is augmented with short profiles of each, as noted below.

- Educator
- Exhibition Staff
- Curator
- Collection Management and Registration Staff
- Information Technology Staff
- Administrative Assistant
- Administrator

- Visitor Services Staff
- Fundraiser
- Conservator
- Marketing/Public Relations/Media Staff
- Earned Income Staff
- Security Staff
- Maintenance Staff
- Financial Staff
- Director
- Other Job Titles

There are three sets of full-time museum jobs. When applying for employment, it is important to know and understand the reasons for and nature of each. There are commonalities, but there are also differences. Each of the jobs mentioned in this chapter can be a new job, an existing job, or a reconfigured job.

The descriptions in this chapter offer an overview of the various job duties available in museums and suggest the personality profiles appropriate for each. More complete and detailed explanations will be contained in actual employment announcements. For comparison purposes when considering a particular job, it is recommended that a prospective employee look at announcements for similar positions at other museums. Government museums are perhaps the easiest to access to study position descriptions and compensation. As with any government post, these are listed regardless of actual openings.

EDUCATOR

Museums educate. Indeed, it is this work that allows them to be tax-exempt, 501(c)3 charitable entities. How they do this, for whom, and why varies widely from institution to institution. It is a unique form of education. In the field it is referred to as "object-based" learning. Things, such as original collection objects, reproductions, interactive installations, and the like, are the vehicles through which museums engage people's interests.

In looking at position descriptions, it is common to see references to classroom teaching experience. Often the word *gallery* is substituted for the word *classroom*. Understanding how people of diverse backgrounds learn is critical for museum educators today. Those backgrounds can be determined by race, ethnicity, age, gender, income, education, place of origin, and/or recognized physical or mental characteristics that may seem to fall outside mainstream norms. Museum education capabilities have been vastly expanded with the advent and application of new information technology (IT) and hands-on interactive mechanisms. (Science museums in particular excel at these.) Therefore, IT knowledge and abilities are now essential skills for those seeking education positions.

Much has been written about the ways people learn in museums. When interviewed, candidates for teaching jobs will no doubt be asked about their knowledge in this regard. If they are not, they should discuss the topic. Given the range of learners that museums attract, no institution wants to fall short when it comes to meeting expectations.

Museum educators should be involved in the full range of public programs a museum offers. This participation should start with concept development, implementation, and assessment for exhibitions, publications, research, and programs for all audiences.

Obviously, a museum educator needs to be a "people person." Introverts avoid this field unless they are working in the background with technology, research, or behind-the-scenes writing. For the public, education personnel are most often seen giving tours as docents, guides, or interpreters in galleries or historic houses and sites. However, much teaching takes place behind the scenes in classrooms or other spaces set aside for these purposes. Figure 2.1 shows a group of students listening to an educator at the Ara Pacis Museum, Rome, Italy, in 2005.

It is important to remember that museum education reaches many ages. Children are an obvious cohort but so, too, are adults, be they retired or still in the workplace. Museums often appeal to specialists in various areas. Attracting these audiences is wise. There is an increasing interest in serving mentally or physically challenged audiences. New methods for engaging this cohort are proving effective. When applying for education positions, candidates must inquire about the breadth of expectations for their work with all audiences.

EXHIBITION STAFF

Exhibitions make up the most public aspect of what museums do. For the average person, museums justify their existence through these communication forums. Exhibitions are what people think of when they think of museums. In figure 2.2, exhibition designer Michael Batista explains an exhibit installation at the Metropolitan Museum of Art to students.

There are a variety of museum staff positions that exist to make exhibits possible. While the intellectual origins of exhibitions are typically the domain of curators and other scholars, creating exhibitions involves talented hands-on enablers. These include designers of several kinds as well as carpenters,

Figure 2.1. School tour listening to educator. Ara Pacis Museum, Rome, Italy, 2005.
Photo by Steven Miller

preparators, and installers. Larger museums have more of these positions and smaller museums have fewer. There are obvious skills required. The academic backgrounds for exhibition staff are often found in the applied arts. Employees will have undergraduate degrees in sculpture, painting, graphics, design, architecture, film, etc. Graduate degrees will include master's in fine arts, architecture, set design, architecture, or virtual technology to name a few. Over time, these degrees will cease to be as important as experience. The exhibition area of a museum is one place where a confirmed record of physical accomplishment is of immense importance when looking for work. Carrying a portfolio to an interview for an exhibition-related job is expected.

Museum exhibition employees are people with keen aesthetic sensibilities. They have what is referred to as a good "eye" regarding how things will appear in a gallery, a publication, a website, or other IT application. They will understand how colors, material finishes, gallery furnishings, etc. can work cohesively in real or virtual space. They will know how video, hands-on interactive, sound, light, etc. will and can fit into an exhibition so that it makes sense and is not distracting, out of place, overpowering, or constantly out of order.

Exhibition staff will be production-oriented and able to plan and execute exhibit concepts in a timely manner and on budget. They must work well with curators, scholars, consultants, administrators, and maintenance staff. Sometimes trustees are involved with exhibitions in an oversight capacity. Candidates need to get a good sense of how museums accomplish this and the role an exhibit designer plays.

If applying for exhibition jobs of the kinds outlined here, be certain to confirm the workspace and equipment available. Exhibitions can be prepared in the places where they will be shown, elsewhere in a museum, or even off-site. Once you know the sorts of exhibitions a museum does, you will know what is needed to accomplish them. For example, a museum of photography

Figure 2.2. Metropolitan Museum of Art exhibition designer Michael Batista explaining an exhibit installation for a Seton Hall University MA Program in Museum Professions student field trip.
Photo by Steven Miller

will presumably have substantial framing needs. Can this be done with existing staff in existing spaces? Is the customary equipment on hand to mat and frame the images to meet a busy exhibit schedule? Who budgets for these costs and how much influence will you have in this process?

CURATOR

Curators are the object specialists of a museum. They are the go-to individuals when people have questions or need information about aspects of the human or natural world their museum collects. The best curators are connoisseurs.

Museum curators are usually specialists in the scholarly aspects of a museum's mission and the objects reflecting that purpose. These people are an institution's brain trust. Regardless of the museum, be it involved in science, history, or art, there is a generally expected scholastic résumé to qualify for these positions. In addition to a BA or BS, a curator will have an MA or MS, and increasingly a PhD. The best curators have impressive academic credentials and accomplishments as well as considerable experience in both obvious and arcane aspects of their museum's intellectual turf. Starting with original objects in their care, they are voracious researchers.

Curatorial job applicants need to convey their specialties in a convincing and enthusiastic manner. Few museums fill these positions with people unfamiliar with whatever sort of collection requires intellectual care. Recognizing that people interviewing curator candidates may be unfamiliar with the job and the subjects the museum is responsible for, applicants need to be experts at selling their expertise.

Increasingly, curators cannot simply hide and pursue whatever individual research they wish. As noted elsewhere in this book, the emphasis museums now place on exhibitions requires curators of all stripes to be *always* planning and executing exhibits—preferably ones that will attract a lot of visitors! These exhibitions include temporary and more long-term exhibitions. A static exhibition schedule is abhorred by museum trustees in particular.

While most curators love the job and tend to stick with it throughout their museum careers, some become directors or move into a management capacity, especially as it relates to collection matters and staffing. While the day of the director/curator is pretty much over in the museum world, having leaders with curatorial experience is usually beneficial.

Getting started as a curator can be a challenge given the length of time curators stay in particular positions, the scarcity of positions desired, and the competition for jobs. Often the best way to start a curatorial track is to take entry-level assistant curatorial positions or curator posts in small regional museums. These offer opportunities to gain experience and develop a portfolio of exhibits, scholarly research, and collection knowledge. These sorts of jobs often allow more freedom and creativity than might be the case in larger museums.

As museums have prospered, so has the role of the consulting curator. These are freelance contract individuals hired for one-time projects. They are especially prominent in contemporary art circles. This type of role can be filled by experienced curators on leave or special assignment (see figure 2.3) but can also provide valuable experience. When developing a curator portfolio while seeking a full-time museum position, this sort of part-time or temporary project-based curating is a good way to build a résumé. Unless there are suspect circumstances preventing a person from being considered for a museum job, prospective employers will understand why an applicant has taken on various temporary curatorial projects while looking for permanent, full-time work.

Figure 2.3. The author, 2011, in his former curatorial department at the Museum of the City of New York for a year-long consulting project with its collection of N. Currier and Currier & Ives prints.
Photo by Sean Corcoran

Please note that curators tend to choose specialties from the beginning of their careers. Thus, curators in American art rarely veer off into Asian art, or natural history collections, or cars. For the purposes of this book, the word *curator* applies only to collection-centered jobs rather than those holding a title of curator of education, history, programs, interpretation, or some other aspect of a museum's internal operating structure.

COLLECTION MANAGEMENT AND REGISTRATION STAFF

When it comes to the responsible stewardship of its collections, whether owned or borrowed, it is essential that a museum: 1) maintain and keep current a professionally accepted cataloging system for these items; 2) know where these items are, including when in transit; and 3) understand their condition. These assignments are usually handled by someone with the title of collection manager or registrar. The employee is the accountant for collections. The personality profile calls for someone who is highly organized, detail oriented, punctilious, focused, systematic, and loves record keeping. In addition to these on-the-job characteristics, the person needs to be able to stand up to supervisors, colleagues, members of a museum's board of trustees, or outsiders who may want to ignore or violate established, professionally sanctioned collection management procedures. Dreamers, insecure schmoozers, or experimenters who suffer from scattered attention spans are ill-suited to the job.

Cataloging collections requires keeping relevant information on record and in a safe place. The museum field has established generally accepted practices and protocols for this. A collection manager's job is to do it. The person may usually not generate the information itself as that is often a curatorial, consultant, or other scholarly pursuit. It can also come with an object in the form of relevant documents or spoken information. There are standard ways of describing things in museum collections. Accuracy is always a cataloging requirement, especially as more and more collections become available online for research or other applications. This Internet access is usually centered in a collection-management office, although it can be in other parts of a museum. Given the changing nature of research and how cultural materials are identified, there will inevitably be changes in catalog information. Deciding who has the final authority in this regard, and who makes the changes, is an essential management decision for a museum.

A critical task for a collection manager or registrar is to keep track of where a museum's collections are. Storage generally falls under the scope of collection management duties. A cardinal museum sin is to not know the locations of what it owns. From the tiniest natural history specimen to the largest history artifact, every accessioned item has to have a designated and recorded home.

A critical collection management assignment is to document and keep track of objects coming into or going out of a museum, as well as what is moving around within it. While much of what a museum collects remains in one place most of the time, collections are not always stationary. Though not conservators, these duties require an understanding of safe ways to handle and contain collections. Successful job candidates will know how to do this.

INFORMATION TECHNOLOGY STAFF

Information technology (IT) feeds everything museums do whether it involves internal operations or external interactions. This reality is the norm for most entities these days. Museum positions are required for servicing the full range of technology including but not limited to computers, exhibition technology (see figure 2.4), social media, and what used to be known as audio-visual applications.

Figure 2.4. Immersion Room, Cooper-Hewitt Smithsonian Design Museum, New York, NY. The touch-screen table allows visitors to select wallpaper samples from the museum's extensive historic collection of wallpapers. Upon activation, the chosen paper design is projected on the four walls of the room.
Photo by Steven Miller

Museums have three challenges when it comes to IT: sustaining technology already in use; keeping up with the latest developments in the field and assessing the appropriateness for various uses on the job; and having non-IT employees technologically capable and comfortable with whatever programs and equipment they must use, or be willing to learn about them. Tracking new technology that is appropriate for museums is an essential task for IT personnel. Those in charge of word and graphic technology will need to be familiar with old programs and systems also, since museums can be havens for equipment that employees love even if woefully out of date. IT personnel also need to watch over outside IT suppliers and consultants and to be familiar with the latest security issues.

People attending to IT can come from within the museum field or outside it. As with many other museum positions, IT operatives can be consulting, part-time, or full-time paid employees. Academic credentials may not be as important for these individuals as for other museum employees. Practical skills and knowledge are what count. These may be absent from a candidate's résumé when seeking a first job in this realm, but in time they will be acquired.

The personality profiles of IT people can resemble a geek with awkward interpersonal abilities. Sheldon Cooper of the television series *The Big Bang Theory* comes to mind. They also speak a language unintelligible to the average museum employee, especially staff with little interest in technology of any sort. For that reason, IT employees will require "handlers" who can help explain, monitor, and instruct both the technology specialist and the ignorant.

Security issues with IT are substantial these days. The importance cannot be underestimated. Security must be understood by all museum staff but especially managers—those directly responsible for IT matters and security personnel. All museum technology should be accessible to designated staff. Most personnel policies now outline who these people are. All museum job applicants should inquire about computer and social media use, access, and security.

Computers are a way of life today, and especially in museums. They are essential for exhibition development and implementation (writing in particular), fundraising, accounting, collection cataloguing, programming of all sorts, public relations, you name it. When they work correctly, do what is needed, and the people operating them are capable, they are great. That is hardly a constant, which is why IT people will always have jobs.

ADMINISTRATIVE ASSISTANT

Administrative assistants used to be called secretaries. The title morphed into what it is now when *secretary* was considered both demeaning and sexist because it was mostly filled by women. The position largely supports museum executives such as directors or division heads. The job involves handling correspondence, both online and off, arranging meetings and appointments, keeping files and confidential information in order, making travel arrangements, and a host of housekeeping measures, all of which are essential to the smooth, timely, and accurate running of an office. Computer literacy is essential and will often be better than what the boss knows. Dictation is pretty much a lost art, but keeping accurate and timely meeting minutes is essential. Boards of trustees may have a titular officer position called secretary, but in my experience these good folks have never done anything secretarial as outlined herein.

The job requires a high level of information security and interpersonal skills. Most administrative assistants report directly to only one person, but sometimes the position is shared. This needs to be clearly explained in job descriptions to avoid, among other problems, inequitable demands put upon an assistant by staff. These employees also need to understand they do not have the power or authority status of their respective bosses. This misunderstanding can sometimes occur.

In a museum context, an administrative assistant need not have a deep (or any) background in museums. Extensive office skills are prized over extensive museum knowledge. Therefore, applicants will be considered from a wide range of experiences. Depending on where a person is in life, this position can be used as a stepping-stone for other museum work or can be a satisfactory job in and of itself. An entry-level employee who is also in graduate school sometimes finds the position helpful for financial, informational, and connectivity reasons.

Formal education requirements for administrative assistants are less rigorous than is the case for conservators, curators, educators, etc. An undergraduate degree is the norm these days because most job applicants have one, but they are not necessarily a requirement. What is necessary is IT knowledge and what would customarily be described as traditional secretarial skills. From a personality perspective, administrative assistants should be extremely organized, dutiful, cheerful, capable, and discreet. This is not a job for a gossip.

ADMINISTRATOR

Not to be confused with administrative assistant, many museums have supervisory managerial positions that exist between rank and file staff and the director. These positions can be heads of departments, divisions, offices, or similar specifically configured operating elements within the larger institution. These positions require management experience as well as knowledge of the subject area of the unit. Overall museum expertise is a plus, although there are some positions where this is less necessary. Directing finance, maintenance, or retail departments come to mind. The positions can be quite important and essential to the smooth operating of a museum, especially a larger one. Titles often start with the words Assistant Director, Managing Director, Director of . . . or, Officer.

Administration positions are often filled from within by employees who wish and are qualified to advance in rank and responsibilities. They are also filled by outside candidates. Lateral employment changes within a museum can happen but only if a person meets requisite qualities and can fit into the different job. Being an existing employee does not guarantee upward internal mobility. Care must be exercised by such candidates to guard against disappointment and avoid undue repercussions by successful outside candidates.

Perhaps the most obvious illustration of administrative divisions found within a larger museum is offered by the Smithsonian Institution. Headquartered in Washington, DC, it has several museums and other components there as well as off site, such as two in New York City.

The personality of an administrator requires calm management abilities, a deep knowledge of the work required for a job, and a willingness to navigate successfully between staff and bosses higher up the food chain. Usually administrators are supported by their bosses but not always or all the time; and, usually administrators support their staff but not always or all the time. When considering such jobs, it is difficult but helpful to ascertain the facts in these regards.

With the exception of maintenance and security administrators, formal education credentials are the norm for administrators. The minimum of an undergraduate degree is common, with graduate degrees customary. A few will even have PhDs. Considerable management experience is essential to succeed as an administrator. Transitioning into a senior-level management position from a less responsible one can be difficult. Training is helpful as are courses in how to manage projects, people, problems, professional expectations, and potential outcomes on the job.

VISITOR SERVICES STAFF

Visitors to museums often judge their experience according to how they are treated by staff. Their encounters can make or break what they think of an institution. A museum can have a fabulous collection, wonderful exhibitions, and a beautiful setting, but if an employee treats them badly, that is what people remember. Visitors are not shy in expressing thoughts regarding a positive or not-so-positive museum experience. This is especially true now with so many online opportunities to review a restaurant, hotel, resort, and, yes, a museum.

Most visitors encounter museum employees on the "front lines." These tend to be people at the admission desk; an information kiosk; answering phones and responding to social media; or working in the sales shop. They can be described under the job category of Visitor Services, though other titles are used.

The main work of Visitor Services personnel is to process admissions and provide information about the museum. Visitors will assume these folks know everything about the place, including not just what exhibitions are on view at the time but what collection item can be seen where; what is scheduled to be on view in the future; where a curator can be found; and how to meet the director. Visitor Services personnel are also the people who receive the most direct complaints about a museum.

Given the vacillating, often transient lives of some staff in these jobs, the positions always need to be filled, which is not always easy. The jobs can be part-time, full-time, seasonal, and even hourly. They often include working weekends and evenings. A lot of shifting occurs as people call in sick, quit, take days off, etc.

The personality of a Visitor Services employee must be outgoing, friendly, patient, and personable without being silly or odd. These individuals need to be physically presentable and socially comfortable dealing with the range of visitors most museums get. They represent not only the museum but often the community the museum is in. To a degree, they are fulfilling the role of the local Chamber of Commerce. Information is their content. After the most popular question, "Where is the rest room?" common questions will include, "Where is a good restaurant?" "How far is it to . . .?" "What other sites do you recommend we visit?"

Given the increased presence of technology in museum exhibits and public programming, familiarity with computers, iPads, cell phone use, camera/video applications, etc. is increasingly necessary. Academic credentials can be helpful, but for many of these positions the requirements are minimal. For museums in major urban centers, knowledge of two or more foreign languages can be advantageous.

FUNDRAISER

Museums are expensive places to operate. Even the wealthiest museum always needs additional income. Almost regardless of size, every museum will have at least one employee whose job involves raising money. Even government-owned and -operated museums need to be mindful of how to get operating and special project funding through elected officials' budgets and established agencies, commissions, programs, etc.

Money to support museums is obtained in several ways. It can be earned through admission fees, renting spaces for events, memberships, and selling items in a shop. It is gotten through grants from foundations, government programs, or corporations. And, it is realized by individual discretionary donations. This last category of funding is by far the most prominent and important when it comes to the consistency and magnitude of financing.

Fundraising in museums is generally referred to as development, although there are other names including advancement, external relations, and philanthropy. Large museums have multi-staffed departments devoted to this work. In looking at job ads, the diversity of talents is clear. Skills can center on foundation research and grant writing, prospect cultivation, membership programming, special events, and soliciting and establishing bequests.

Fundraising as a unique profession involves a range of learning opportunities and requirements. There are courses one can, and should, take, but there is no substitute for on-the-job training. Getting into fundraising can happen through entry-level, part-time, seasonal, or project jobs that will teach aspects of the work.

It is important to note that being a professional fundraiser allows for many employment options. The experience gained when raising money at a college, museum, hospital, or any other nonprofit entity can often be applied elsewhere. While it might be preferable to have fundraising staff that specialize in getting money for museums, it is not always a hiring requirement.

The personality profile of fundraising staff will show a love of research and data sifting, an ability to suggest how certain people might be connected to an organization, patience with having requests denied, and knowing that few others associated with the organization know anything about how to raise money . . . or want to. There are many misconceptions about nonprofit fundraising. Those who do it must be confident as well as confidential in their work.

The subject of people (meaning donors or prospective donors when it comes to museums) and their money is an enormously sensitive one. Much of what is discussed in fundraising circles is nobody's business except those involved in a private conversation.

Most museum fundraisers have at least an undergraduate degree. Many have graduate degrees. The subject of these studies is rarely fundraising, although that is beginning to change. Few people really know what development staff do. Consequently, a major part of the job is explaining it to others, especially trustees. All too often certain people in authority at museums assume fundraisers will bring in all the money an institution needs, alone. This is a fallacy that has to be regularly addressed on the job.

Finally, the chief fundraisers for museums have to be the director and the board of trustees. These people may or may not embrace this reality well, if at all. The vast majority of development personnel do not actually ask directly for money, especially of individuals; they will work through the board of trustees and the director who will make "the ask."

CONSERVATOR

A first priority for any museum is to assure the good physical care of its collections. This happens in several ways including direct actions taken on an object, assuring it is safely housed, and protecting it from undue access or use. *Conservation* is the overall word for such work. Figure 2.5 shows an example of an art conservation lab.

Museum conservators are people who physically interact with museum collections for their benefit. This is a rarified and exacting profession with a variety of academic and manual skill requirements. It is usually divided according to certain material characteristics common to museum collections. Thus, there are conservators for paintings, paper-based art, ceramics, wood, metal, etc. A new

Figure 2.5. Museum studies students visiting an art conservation lab.
Photo by Steven Miller

area for time-based art has recently been introduced. This involves preserving virtual and IT art, created for the Internet and other applications and use.

Being a museum conservator requires an unusual mix of intellectual interests, physical abilities, and academic qualifications. Manual dexterity is a must. A background in science (chemistry) is essential. Depending on the sorts of material evidence one works with, knowledge of various kinds of art, historic artifacts, or scientific specimens is necessary.

Personality qualities for conservators involve being intellectually curious, patient, cautious, punctilious, and confident about one's intellect *and* manual abilities. This is hardly a field that does things in a hurry unless an emergency calls for swift corrective or safety measures to secure cultural materials. In those cases, further corrective work that needs to be performed on objects will happen later under specified lab conditions.

The best way to become acquainted with museum conservation is to join the AIC, the America Institute for Conservation of Historic and Artistic Works (http://www.conservation-us.org). Getting into the conservation field requires graduate study, and there are various rigorous programs listed on the AIC website. It demands specific academic qualifications and hands-on training. Being accepted for internships with qualified museum conservation labs or private practitioners will be part of your training plan. It is important to note that this aspect of museum work cannot be pursued by amateurs or part-time aficionados. While other museum staff, notably curators and collection managers, will have an affinity for conservation, few if any are qualified to practice conservation.

There are two ways of practicing as a conservator: get a job with a museum or set up a freelance business. Most large museums, especially art museums, have conservation departments. They will have specialists for the various material things represented in the museum's collections, especially paintings, works on paper, and decorative arts objects. Private businesses are usually individual conservators. They, too, will specialize in particular material objects, along the lines of museums. Most of the work done by private practice conservators is for individuals and commercial galleries. Some museums may accept outside work (for pay), but policies vary from institution to institution. There are also nonprofit conservation centers. These are important for museums that cannot afford individual conservators. The Williamstown Art Conservation Center, Williamstown, MA, is a good example.

MARKETING/PUBLIC RELATIONS/MEDIA STAFF

Promoting exhibitions, acquisitions, scholarship discoveries, staff changes, funding successes, expansions and gallery renovations, and programs of all sorts must be a ceaseless museum endeavor these days. This reflects the highly competitive race for notoriety that museums find themselves in now.

Most museums of any size have positions devoted to marketing and public relations. Marketing is the overall philosophy of why and how a museum will approach explaining itself to the general public and specific audiences and individuals. Public relations embrace how marketing is practiced. Media comprise the many ways used to get the word out.

Initiating and sustaining successful museum public relations profiles is a ceaseless task. Occasionally it involves defending a museum during a controversy. This might be the result of an unpopular deaccessioning, a hiring debate, an acquisition imbroglio, or an exhibition controversy. Fortunately, most of the time museum news is always good news.

People responsible for museum marketing need to be optimistic, outgoing, creative, opportunistic, and enthusiastic. They must be savvy regarding how best to get the word out about an institution's achievements. They also need to have a sense of what is newsworthy. It is essential to have good relationships with the press, be it local, national, or even international (for example, see figure 2.6, which shows a TV interview with Mr. and Mrs. Yogi Berra at

Figure 2.6. WWOR Channel 9 news interview with Mr. and Mrs. Yogi Berra, at the Yogi Berra Museum & Learning Center, Little Falls, NJ.
Photo by Steven Miller

the Yogi Berra Museum & Learning Center). Social media expertise is of the utmost importance now. In addition to knowing how to get positive attention on a regular basis for the general media, museum marketing employees must know about specialty audiences and individuals with interests in particular aspects of a museum.

Museum media personnel need to know how to explain often arcane and specialty subjects to a general audience. And, this usually has to happen quickly. Being a skilled wordsmith is a valued skill. The academic backgrounds for museum media staff may or may not include undergraduate degrees in public relations, marketing, communications, advertising, or media in general.

EARNED INCOME STAFF

Museums have become adept at the commerce of raising money. What were once considered gauche or unseemly business ventures for altruistic institutions are now readily accepted, encouraged, and expected. Would a museum ever consider not having a gift shop these days (see figure 2.7)? What about renting spaces for parties and events? Museums are now central participants in the tourism industry and hope to attract tour groups galore. Creating and selling reproductions of things in a museum's collections is common practice. And, of course, charging admission is customary, at least for private, nongov-

Figure 2.7.   Sales shop, James A. Michener Art Museum, Doylestown, PA, 2018.
Photo by Steven Miller

ernment, museums. The commercial activities of museums are integral parts of an institution's annual revenue stream. Budgets rely on this income.

Positions responsible for assuring profit margins include sales shop managers and staff, rental coordinators, rights and reproductions employees, group tour leaders, and admission personnel. Entry-level positions are always of a front-line nature and often part-time and for weekend service. These are the employees one sees behind the cash register in a museum gift shop or at the admission desk. Employees who administer these areas usually have their own offices behind the scenes, although it is not uncommon to see them filling in when vacancies occur.

The academic background and training desired for museum earned-income positions will vary but largely reflect experience in retail sales, the events rental industry, or the tourism field. Work in museums may or may not be required when being considered for these jobs. Once on the job, though, learning about museums generally and the one in which you work has to happen quickly.

There is a reason why museums are not-for-profit entities. They do not and cannot survive on earned income alone. This reality must be understood by those in authority and especially boards of trustees. The pressure to make money can be severe. When it does not happen, those who are supposed to make that money are let go. This is obviously unfair because the equation is unfair. Regardless, anyone seeking museum work of an earned-income nature must ask what the expectations are and who sets them. Also, prospective employees should ask what happens if expectations are not met?

Regardless of the profitability of a museum's earned-income potential, no institution should ignore possibilities. Attracting tour groups is beneficial. Allowing for event rentals that do not endanger an institution's collections, facilities, staff, operations, etc. can prove valuable. Selling copies of images in a collection can be helpful. People in charge of these duties must be entrepreneurial and creative audience-focused retailers.

SECURITY STAFF

Museum security extends to protecting collections, people (public and staff), and buildings and grounds. There are a range of positions for these duties. Larger museums will hire more people for this than smaller museums. A museum knows its security measures are successful when no collections are stolen or damaged, no persons are hurt or killed in ways that could have been obviously avoided, and responses to natural or human-made disasters are swift, correct, and helped reduce or eliminate unfortunate consequences.

Security coverage starts with people but extends to all sorts of technological applications. These can be seen in galleries with surveillance cameras. Objects on display are often shown in locked display cases, behind bulletproof glass, on pedestals and stanchioned-off from direct access (see figure 2.8). Locks provide obvious intrusion impediments. Gates and other property barriers are essential protective measures. Then, there are the IT safety measures such as passwords, access codes, registration mechanisms, etc. as well as who is allowed access to what machines, computers, and facilities, when, and under what, if any, supervision.

Figure 2.8. Security guard protecting *The Scream* by Edvard Munch, 1893. Note the Plexiglas display container as well as the floor line viewers are instructed not to cross.
Photo by Steven Miller

Security staff may or may not come from within the museum field. They play an interesting role vis-à-vis the rest of a museum's employees. They need to be friendly but watchful, informative but able to keep confidences. The personalities of security personnel can range from pleasant to taciturn. Because dishonesty can happen with a staff person, security employees need to consider any and all eventualities.

Entry-level security positions tend to be on the gallery guard level or for hard-to-fill positions such as night guard when a museum is closed. These usually call for no management or supervisory duties. Higher levels for security do involve management experience. At the top, it is not unusual to find retired military, emergency service, or law enforcement people who want to continue working.

Academic credentials for security staff are often minimal as the skills required fall outside customary school curricula. To be sure, there are undergraduate courses in security and graduate classes are available, but for the most part, the career unfolds on the job. Keeping up with new security measures requires continued training for staff.

Given the value of museum collection items, in addition to securing them physically on the premises, they need to be guarded virtually to help avoid exchanges of fakes for the real thing or outright theft through diversionary measures. Security of collections in transit is of critical importance. This can be a special challenge because the movement is often not under the supervision of the owning museum.

MAINTENANCE STAFF

Inside or outside, museums present a wide range of maintenance challenges. Because so many museums are in old buildings, the difficulties can be especially pronounced. Keeping museums in safe, attractive, and proper operating order is a constant duty (see figure 2.9). Systems and structures always need to be sustained, improved, fixed, and otherwise attended to in responsible ways. Employees hired for this work must understand electrical, plumbing, IT, mechanical systems, and the nature of various building materials.

Most maintenance staff may not come from within the museum field. That is not necessarily a deficit. Many of these individuals will be in their jobs for a very long time. If they are effective, this is positive; if they are not, difficulties will arise. Most other museum personnel are either uninformed, ill-informed, or out of the loop when it comes to the full range of museum maintenance requirements and realities. This can lead to egregious deferred maintenance problems, unreasonable demands and expectations, or acting on improper advice.

Figure 2.9. The Solomon R. Guggenheim Museum, New York, NY, is closed on Thursdays. This is the opportune time for more than simple housekeeping of the main public areas, such as the entrance on Fifth Avenue.

Photo by Steven Miller

Maintenance employees are the people who quite literally do the heavy lifting. They are part of the front-line cleaning crew and are thus essential to how the public perceives a museum. The nature of their interactions with staff and the public will vary depending on their jobs or particular projects and assignments. As with all museum staff, maintenance folks need to be respectful of colleagues. Perhaps even more importantly non-maintenance staff need to be respectful of the people who clean the bathrooms, vacuum offices, repair systems, load and unload supplies and materials, and build or dismantle things. Without these workers, museums would literally fall apart.

Academic credentials are rarely as important for maintenance staff as is experience and practical knowledge and relevant skills. No one demands that a carpenter have a PhD. Getting a job in museum maintenance can happen through entry-level openings or by responding to advertisements for a plumber, electrician, or the aforementioned carpenter position. These announcements are rarely found in museum profession listings. They may be found in local job announcements or on museum websites. Word of mouth is also a conduit, though beware of recommendations by people who are simply supporting an unqualified friend seeking work.

Maintenance job titles vary and include housekeeper, custodian, janitor, technician, groundskeeper, laborer, engineer, head of buildings and grounds, and maintenance supervisor. They need to be on call in varying capacities to deal with emergencies and be on duty for special events that fall outside customary daytime work schedules. In some museums these are union positions.

FINANCIAL STAFF

People responsible for financial matters in a museum are usually identified as an accountant, controller, bookkeeper, comptroller, or chief financial officer. These employees track numbers: income and expenses, tax reports, investments, salaries, benefits, contract agreements (such as tracking grants), budget reports, annual audits, etc. They may also be the HR (Human Resources) office and keep personal files and tabulate attendance, vacation, and personal and sick day records.

There is a distinct personality type for persons involved in this work. They must be detail oriented to the extreme, accurate to a fault, and able to provide numerical information in a timely, confidential, and helpful manner. Slipshod performances allowing multiple interpretations based on incomplete or questionable content are forbidden. Certainly, there can be nuances, opinions, and adjustments to whatever is presented in balance sheets, budget projections, audits, and other financial reports, but these changes tend to reflect the input of content people rather than be caused by the tabulators.

As with several other museum positions, financial slots need not always be filled with people having extensive museum experience. Work in the nonprofit sector is beneficial, as is an understanding of how to navigate widely variable personalities on the job— more than a few of whom don't understand fiscal matters, or care. Moreover, working patiently and productively with boards of trustees is an essential skill. For instance, in museums, for most people, the word *collections* defines the catalogued art, artifacts, or specimens owned rather than outstanding bills or invoices requiring payment collection.

Finance people will have undergraduate degrees reflecting their skills. Graduate degrees will usually be MBAs for finance, accounting, human resources, investments, banking, and the like. They will need to be willing to learn new ways of accounting that may be required when laws change or accounting standards are altered. They need to know about pension plans and health benefits. They must understand tax regulations for staff, contractors, consultants, etc. Experience with annual audits is essential.

Often, personnel manuals describe what is permitted and not permitted regarding finance office activities and access for staff. Job candidates may want to ask about these protective measures though perhaps toward the end of an interview or in a second one, if that occurs.

Candidates for finance positions at museums will probably meet with a trustee or two from the finance sector in an interview. These people are usually of great value as they speak the "same language" as the candidate. Other museum staff positions are rarely familiar enough with a museum finance office to truly understand what happens in it, why, or how. Few museum offices require the utmost extensive confidentialities of finance offices. Unlike other museum positions, this one demands the utmost confidentiality regarding the information it holds and the access thereto.

DIRECTOR

The job of museum director is unique. Oddly, little is written within the museum field about this position, especially by directors. This is unfortunate. It would be helpful for practitioners to explain the work from the inside insofar as what it requires, involves, demands, and how it stands apart from other museum employment. Job descriptions are helpful, but they are usually so all-encompassing as to verge on the ridiculous. They explain the obvious: manage everything perfectly; raise all the money required to run the place;

be a stellar community leader; make the museum stand out above all other museums; be all things to all people; etc. I am hardly being facetious.

In the mid-1990s, there was great turmoil in the ranks of museum directors. People came and went with alarming regularity. In 1994, Paul Goldberger, the *New York Times* art and culture critic, commenced an article on the problem with a tongue-in-cheek generic classified ad:

> Wanted: Charming, erudite executive with the diplomatic skills of a foreign services officer, the financial skills of an investment banker, and the social skills of a 1950s wife. Position requires the academic background of a serious scholar, with the willingness to let most of this knowledge go unused in favor of poring over budgets and staffing issues. Long hours, low pay and the chance to see your name in the papers every time you make even the slightest wrong move.[1]

Most museum positions have verifiable singular skills. Indeed, each job could be described as a specific sort of craft. Museum director positions are different. This is because of the vast range of expectations on the part of employees, trustees, those with some special interest in some aspect of the museum, and the general public. To say that museum directors are institutional traffic cops stationed at busy cultural crossroads would be a woeful understatement. They are the point people for leadership—head honchos who must account for everything and be accountable for everything. Their work is of a 24/7 nature. Good ones are always on call.

Essentially, museum directors are responsible for what I call the seven Ps: planning, promotion, projects, people, professionalism, problems, and potential. Good ones are hard to find. Excellent ones are rare. The management scope is responsible for all work of the positions outlined in this book *but* with the added dimension of trustee stewardship. Most staff report to a single boss. Museum directors report to boards of trustee and thus have multiple bosses. Each of these bosses can have his or her own perspective on what a director should do, how, when, where, and why.

Directors are expected to have distinguished scholarly backgrounds and achievements, but they must be managerial-experienced community leaders. Scholarly interests are difficult to pursue when running a museum of any size. The structural character of museum directing jobs means the hiring process for them is often more drawn out, unpredictable, and wacky than that encountered in ordinary museum hiring. Seeking and getting a museum directing job can be far more nuanced, intense, quixotic, and unpredictable than the steps leading to other museum positions. Everything discussed in this book is valid when seeking the job of museum director, yet much of it is either rudimentary or has minor direct relevance for the particular circumstances of a particular search.

Candidates for museum directing jobs will be well versed in the museum field generally, and the specifics of management, administration, fundraising, community politics, and productive interpersonal relations for cultural institutions. They will also be knowledgeable about the subject of the museum they wish to lead. Unless they are new to the museum field, their résumés will be extensive and even complex. They will have an established record of accomplishment. On occasion a museum board of trustees will hire someone with either no museum experience or very little. For the most part, this decision nearly always results in failure and the job is soon open again.

Director position candidates will either already have directing experience or will be ready to start based on current or previous management positions. Unless a director is hired from within a museum, the process will take far longer than for other museum positions. This is because of the job's complexity and importance, and the fact that trustees do the hiring, and as volunteers, their personal or professional schedules are very full.

Museums seek directors in two ways: they conduct the search themselves, or they hire search firms. The outcome for a director search is the same. It will take time and the candidate must be prepared for the odd twist or turn in the process. The final decision will be conveyed from the search firm or the museum. In the meantime, applicants must be patient and keep everything confidential, with the hope that the museum and the search firm will do the same.

For the most part museums try to hire people suitable for a job, or people whom they feel have potential to grow. An astonishing exception to this logical approach happens with some director searches—but, that is another story.

OTHER JOB TITLES

Occasionally museums create jobs that are not obvious in their titles. A recent random sampling include: Experience Designer, Project Coordinator, Resource Protection Officer, and Director of Engagement. Be on the lookout for new job titles that may or may not describe the job, such as Senior Content Strategist, Director of Engagement, or Floor Supervisor. If nothing else, museums are managerially creative. This practice will muddle along, though the core duties reflected in the above job list will remain in place as museums continue to set and meet mission goals and obligations in customary ways.

CONCLUSION

The more familiar a candidate is with the position she or he applies for, the better. That familiarity should go well beyond a job's generic nature and how it might be defined in the museum field generally. You must try to know what actually will be required, and how that can be accomplished within the hiring museum. Understanding your qualifications and capabilities in the context of an institution and your personality, will assure a more positive application experience.

NOTE

1. Paul Goldberger, "ART: Doesn't Anybody Want This Job?" *New York Times*, Arts & Leisure, June 26, 1994, https://www.nytimes.com/1994/06/26/arts/art-doesn-t -anybody-want-this-job.html.

Chapter Three

Selecting a Museum

As previously discussed, museums are devoted to an incredible array of subjects. They exist in all sizes and configurations. Content varies widely. Missions are diverse, to say the least. When thinking about jobs, it is imperative that you have a good sense of what you prefer among the options. It is equally important to know what you do not want. The process of elimination is as important as the process of selection.

In seeking work, honestly assess your interests and capabilities. Do you have the requisite qualifications, skills, and aptitude for a particular job? Will this be apparent to an employer throughout the application process? Who might your competition be? Where are you in your career trajectory? Does a particular position really appeal to you? Are you ready to be both flexible and opportunistic? The more you know about yourself, the more others can know about you.

We must be realistic about our capabilities. A research biologist from a natural history museum would hardly be a viable candidate for the position of curator of contemporary art. Conversely a curator of contemporary art would make a lousy curator of ichthyology. To be sure, museums have made hiring choices that mystify the outside world as well as the museum field, but these are exceptions. Errors of employment selection inevitably surface. You want to avoid being an incorrectly successful candidate.

This chapter is about how to select a museum to which to apply for a job. It is based on everything from the prospective employee's background (e.g., education) and geographic preference, to museum size and ownership. All involves research. The considerations are

- Museum Disciplines
- Museum Size and Physical Premises

- Museum Life Cycles
- Museum Ownership
- Location, Location, Location
- Research the Museum

MUSEUM DISCIPLINES

Museums tend to divide themselves into several distinct subject areas. Selecting from among them can narrow the scope of your interest and capability prospects. These align with three academic disciplines.

- History
- Science
- Art

Prominent examples of each category are easy to cite. History museums would include the New-York Historical Society, the Smithsonian National Museum of American History, and the West Point Museum. Impressive art museums are the Metropolitan Museum of Art, the National Gallery of Art, and the Denver Art Museum. Science museums would include the American Museum of Natural History, the Science Museum of Minnesota, and the Arizona Museum of Natural History.

Occasionally museums blend two or three of the topics listed above. The Albany Museum of History and Art obviously features two museum academic types; the Maine State Museum presents the history as well as the natural history of the state; and the Carnegie Museums of Pittsburgh embrace art and science. Children's museums are often amalgamations of museum disciplines all geared for younger audiences. And there are cultural centers or performing arts composites that have museum segments. The Smithsonian Institution is an ideal national leader in this regard.

Apply only for jobs in museums whose subjects interest you and for which your résumé and experience is relevant. Considering institutions outside your area of personal or academic enthusiasm is a waste of everyone's time. The need to find work may tempt you to seek and even accept a job to which you will not be fully committed. This indifference will be quickly apparent in a sluggish performance and ultimately work against your career. There are exceptions to be sure. Working as a museum sales shop associate may be the same regardless of a museum's subject. Similar commonalities hold in the area of maintenance and security. Nevertheless, a belief in the value and importance of a museum's subject always leads to heightened employee satisfaction.

MUSEUM SIZE AND PHYSICAL PREMISES

The size of a museum may or may not be of interest to a job seeker, but it is something to consider nonetheless. It will be important for an educator to know about expectations to offer public programs in more than one place regularly or seasonally. Curators need to know where collections are housed and exhibited. Security staff must understand the scope of their duties throughout a museum, be it one building or more. Fundraisers must have a sense of what they must, can, or would like to raise money for. Museums come in different sizes, shapes, and conditions.

Size

- Large
- Medium
- Small

Premises—Number of Buildings

- Single building
- Multiple buildings
- Components of larger often unaffiliated spaces

Premises—Condition of Buildings

- Old
- New
- Renovated

Regardless of a museum's subject, individual jobs will singularly, or in some combined manner, reflect the customary list of positions explained in chapter 2. This is obvious in each classified notice. An important aspect of any position being applied for will be how resources are shared and prioritized. This may be especially critical with museums of mixed disciplines. For example, at some of the institutions cited above, does natural history, art, or history get priority over the other subject contained in the museum's title? If so, what effect will that have on or for a job you seek?

Museums exist in an astonishing array of physical manifestations. Most are in single buildings devoted only to that purpose. Some are vast with large landholdings and scores of buildings, as is the case with Colonial Williamsburg, VA, or Historic Deerfield, MA. Smaller museums can be found in structures that exist for other purposes, as is the case with the American Folk Art Museum in New York City. Do you want to work in one building or many?

Remember, when it comes to museums, one size does not fit all. When considering a job, look at the museum as reflecting these easily defined characteristics. Think about your preferences, or if you even have any.

Large Museums

Some people would prefer to work in large organizations, while others prefer small ones. There are pros and cons. Job applicants need to assess options. Large museums have what appear to be adequate and experienced personnel systems, support staff, leadership, facilities, and well-established positions. Employees may be small fish in big ponds. Bureaucracy, habits, and procedural requirements may stifle initiative, creativity, independence, and speedy accomplishments, but learning how things are done, in mostly positive ways, in a large museum can be of immense value for entry-level professionals. Working for a large organization can be impressive for one's reputation. Presumably colleagues are highly regarded. Also, benefits can be very good.

Medium-Size Museums

A medium-size museum may have an operating budget of between $800,000 and $2 million. There may be five to fifteen paid staff, though not necessarily on duty year-round or full-time. There will be a professional staff structure with supervisors and reporting positions. The museum can easily be operated according to generally accepted professional standards. Employees will have multiple assignments, which gives staff chances to learn outside their comfort zones but can also be disruptive when trying to focus on single responsibilities. These museums cost less to run but every dollar counts; there is little budget wiggle room.

Small Museums

Small museums usually have budgets under $800,000 and, at most, eight or fewer staff. These positions may be seasonal and part-time. Small museums tend to rely on volunteers to meet needs otherwise handled by paid professionals. Small museums can be as professional as their larger kin. Size deficiencies are compensated for in the freedom employees have to expand their authority to include more variety and focus more on what they want to do, when and how they want to do it. Being a big fish in a small pond can have its advantages. You will certainly be more noticeable within the organization and outside it too, if you want. You will get more diverse experience, and probably faster than in a larger museum. This can help your résumé if and when you seek another job to advance your career.

Physical Premises

Regardless of the job, museum employees need appropriate and adequate facilities in which to pursue their work. Space in particular can be a challenge if it is inadequate, in poor condition, and/or must be shared in ways that interfere with one's productivity. As noted elsewhere, given the idiosyncratic origins and applications of museums, interior space usage for staffing swings from logical to confusing. Job candidates are advised to see their work areas in advance of accepting (or even applying for) a job. This usually isn't possible until an interview, but it doesn't hurt to try. If a person is applying for a position within his or her museum, presumably job facilities are known. Sometimes outside candidates can learn about the physical arrangements of a job in advance from colleagues.

When hunting for work, know the age and operating condition of the premises you will be working in. Age can be deceptive because while a founding year may seem old, a current building might have been built, or moved into, later. The New-York Historical Society dates to 1804, but it did not start at its current building at Central Park West and 77th Street. The Frick Collection in New York City is a museum in a building that was once a private residence. Working with and around this history can be variously fun or frustrating. Sticking with New York City examples, the Metropolitan Museum of Art has grown dramatically since it first appeared at its current location in Central Park. Maintenance employees deal with complex infrastructure systems to keep the place operating. A recent date of museum origin implies new systems, staffing, governance, and facilities. While this may suggest all is copacetic, depending on what was done, how, and why, may mean the reality ranges from exciting to frustrating.

It is not unusual for museums to be in multiple buildings. Buildings may be within close proximity or scattered far and wide. Historic New England has a collection of several dozen properties throughout six states. There are support structures for offices and collections. Colonial Williamsburg is a large town. The Western Reserve Historical Society has an archipelago of connected buildings in Cleveland, plus Hale Farm and Village in Akron. The Philadelphia Museum of Art operates several sites in that city. Even museums that appear to have only one structure may have others to meet storage and operating needs. The Maine State Museum has a support center for collection storage and the archeology department a few miles south of its main building. Understanding the physical scope of a museum is important for job applicants if their position will involve working in more than one location, or being responsible for aspects of more than one location.

MUSEUM LIFE CYCLES

As with most institutions, not to mention people and businesses, museums have life cycles. These are predictable. Job candidates are advised to understand and proceed as they think best according to personal and professional options and preferences. Museum life cycles depend on why they were formed; how they have sustained or changed their mission; where they are located; what strengths and weaknesses have contributed (are contributing) to successes or failures; how their community has supported them in the past; and what is the present situation in that regard (define community as you think best, it is often plural); what is the nature of current staffing and leadership; and, of course, what is the financial condition of the place.

With the absence of one major stage, museum life cycles parallel those of businesses. Looking to the corporate sector can be instructive when seeking museum employment. You could even ask at an interview where staff and leadership think the museum is in its life. The one major stage that is generally absent in museum life cycles is closure. Museums rarely cease to exist as most companies eventually do. It happens, but usually they shrink, merge, move, or change missions. For some reason museums seem to survive almost in spite of themselves.

There are five museum life cycles.

- Long-Established Museums
- Museums in Formation
- New Museums
- Changing Museums
- Failing Museums

Long-Established Museums

Most museum job seekers will be approaching institutions that have been around for a while. Their histories are worth learning about prior to applying for work or interviewing. Presumably they are established in their mission, operations, reputation, and professionalism. In addition to the museums listed elsewhere, others would include the Museum of the City of New York; the Museum of Fine Arts, Boston; the American Museum of Natural History, New York, NY; the Chicago Historical Society; and the Mississippi Museum of Natural Science, Jackson, MS. The list is long and getting longer year by year.

On occasion, museums of long-standing existence will experience problems. This was certainly the case with the New-York Historical Society in the mid-1980s when it almost closed. The museum dates from 1804. It was rescued with the intervention of the New York State Attorney General's office and the financial support of several wealthy individuals. It is now doing very well. Fortunately, for the most part, such institutional glitches are exceptions. Unless it is an experimental position or funded temporarily, whatever job you apply for at a museum of some age will probably exist for a long time.

Once hired by a long-established museum, an employee must deal with past legacies and current workplace practices while deciding what needs to be done to go forward. Preparing for this circumstance can begin at an interview or even before, with preparatory candidate research. How much of an influence will previous work have on your work? In most cases that influence will be positive and why you want the job!

Most museum employees are part of a personnel continuum. How will you fit into that? Who is there and why, who went before you, and what will you be doing for the present and going forward? Because they are group efforts and have been largely a community engaged over the years, established museums are oddly referential in their reputations. Staff, trustees, volunteers, and the community at large have long memories which may or may not influence current goals, objectives, and activities. Those memories can be peculiarly specific.

A negative possibility when working at a museum that has been in existence for a long time can unfold when someone wants to make radical changes. These can happen with unprecedented collection retention or acquisition decisions, programming alterations, personnel overhauls, physical alterations, or moves. Over time museums can become beloved local institutions. Substantial alterations of personnel, content, physical structure, programs, etc. are not always greeted with joy.

When looking at a job or jobs within museums of longevity, be certain you understand what is on the institutional agenda going forward. For instance, it may be wonderful to be part of change, or it may be upsetting—especially if you were unaware of the magnitude of any change underway.

Museums in Formation

Joining the staff of a museum still forming can be exciting. You are getting in on the ground floor (sometimes literally) of an institution as it creates itself. Naturally, when considering this sort of job, you will need to know your role and how that may or may not change going forward. What authority will you have to do what? Who will you report to and will that person or those people be around for a while? What are their backgrounds and qualifications? Most importantly, what is the mission of the prospective museum? Who set the mission and why? In your mind, does it have merit and does it appeal to you? Is the whole project financially viable? Do you understand the plan? What is the timetable, and how does that conform to your career plans? Does the job appear fairly secure, or is it temporary, or an experiment? If you are interested in growing with the pending museum, will that be possible? At the time of this writing a good example of a museum in formation is the Lucas Museum of Narrative Art being built in Los Angeles, CA.

New Museums

New museums are often ideal places to seek employment. When they open to the public and undergo an operating shakedown period, job openings can occur more frequently than with established institutions. Moreover, job adjustments often cause the creation of new or renewed positions. Two good examples of new museums are the National Museum of African American History and Culture on the Mall in Washington, DC, and the Museum of the American Revolution, in Philadelphia, PA.

Applicants to new museums need to ask the same sorts of interview questions they would for museums in formation. New museums are founded on certain expectations. If those include projected attendance figures, the success of education programs, or retail trade activity, the reality of how those are unfolding is important to know. Fortunately, there are fewer unrealistic projections for museum attendance and income expectations than was once the case. However, be alert for any indication that visitation will be a critical factor in assessing employee performance.

Museum job seekers should look for employment that will use their talents to best advantage, help them grow professionally, and provide adequate compensation. It is also ideal if the position allows for creative opportunities. Those might include adjusting the work to meet unanticipated needs, expanding the scope of the museum's initial expectations, and embracing larger goals and objectives. Professional engagement on a variety of fronts could make a job far more interesting than expected. There might be a better chance of this sort of personal reward with a new or anticipated museum than a pre-existing one.

Changing Museums

Occasionally a museum will be in flux as it changes its mission, operation, content, place, governing structure, etc. in some very substantial manner. The reasons may be self-motivated and positive, caused by internal difficulties, or forced upon it by outside influences. Presumably job applicants will be more than aware of the anticipated alterations. Positions will or may be enormously affected by the alterations underway, while others could be marginally impacted.

An example of a museum that is changing a central aspect of its mission is the Berkshire Museum in Pittsfield, MA. In an interest to focus on science and history, it is ending its art concentrations. To achieve this, the board is deaccessioning by sale art of exceptional value. The idea has caused an enormous public debate. Presumably anyone applying for a job at a museum experiencing this sort of change will research what is happening and why, and how that may affect any work being applied for.

Failing Museums

Museums rarely fail. When they do, it was because they were poorly established to begin with and did not have the resources and passionate leadership to succeed, or an unexpected tragedy has befallen them such as the death of a key leader or the sudden absence of a major funding source. It is hard to predict museum failures, but when seeking work, the more research a candidate can do with this possibility in mind the better.

On occasion a failing museum is saved by being taken over by another institution. Fortuitous examples of this can be found in the distant past, but more recent examples are unfolding. The future will probably see more. From an employment perspective, certain staff positions will segue to the absorbing museum while others will be lost.

Two recent sad examples of failing museums were the American Textile History Museum in Lowell, MA, and the Corcoran Gallery of Art in Washington, DC. Both have closed because of a lack of funding. As noted, museums are expensive places to operate, and many live almost a hand-to-mouth existence financially. In spite of gnawing fiscal realities, few museums go out of business. Nevertheless, anyone looking for museum work must assess the health of an institution's balance sheet.

Some museums that are on the brink of disaster survive by merging with or being taken over by another museum. Recent examples indicate that when done responsibly the results are successful. The mission of the weak museum is strengthened by a healthier museum. Collections usually survive in good hands. Knowledgeable employees remain albeit at another institution. The public continues to benefit.

Examples of museum takeovers are the now-closed Higgins Armory Museum, Worcester, MA, the collections of which are now in the Worcester Art Museum, and the defunct Academy of Natural Sciences of Philadelphia, which is now the Academy of Natural Sciences of Drexel University. Such situations do not happen quickly. Given the open nature of the American museum world, job seekers can or should be able to learn about possible major changes at museums where work is sought before deciding to apply for a job in them.

MUSEUM OWNERSHIP

It is important to understand museum ownership and its ramifications for a job you seek. Generally, ownership can fall into one of the following categories. Sometimes there might be a blend.

- Individually owned museums
- Private nonprofit charities
- Government-owned museums (town, city, county, state, national, including military)
- Company museums
- Academic museums: college or university
- Museum facilities owned by a larger entity

Museums can be owned in one of several ways. Prospective employees should understand the impact ownership will have on a job. Institutional missions, reporting structures, public access, and financial arrangements may vary depending on museum ownership.

Individually Owned Museums

Occasionally a museum will be owned by an individual or a family. It usually houses a collection(s) of personal interest to him, her, or them. The mission reflects one perspective. Working in this sort of museum will mean answering to a single direction, whim, desire, idea, hope, and purpose. The influence of one ego will be the deciding management philosophy. Of course, if ownership is shared, there can be ego clashes. Job applicants must be mindful of the sort of workplace atmosphere this kind of museum can engender. A good current example is Magazzino Italian Art, in Cold Spring, NY. It is the private collection of a husband and wife team devoted to the Arte Povera movement in Italy. There seem to be two eventual destinies for these museums: they close or become more typically governed museum entities. Automobile museums seem to particularly suffer the former affliction.[1,2]

Private Nonprofit Charities

As previously explained the vast majority of museums in America are private tax-exempt charities "owned" by no one individual or larger body. They are self-supporting, self-operating entities, usually governed by self-perpetuating boards of trustees. That body may have other names, but the role is the same. It is the fiduciary body for the museum, and members have volunteered to support the need. Similar boards exist for a raft of other nonprofit institutions including colleges, hospitals, animal shelters, libraries, symphony orchestras, food banks, etc. This civic profile is almost unique to the United States. In the rest of the world, these public benefits are generally owned and operated by governments.

It is not unusual for private museums to have ancillary volunteer groups organized to support the institution financially. The most common name for these is the "Friends of the XYZ Museum." Much of what they do involves events and especially the organizing of annual gala parties for which tickets are sold and underwriting is sought. From an employee perspective, it is important to understand how those involved with a Friends group interact with and manage their relations with the museum they support. It is far too easy for conflicts to arise.

People seeking work at private museums need to be assured they are well run, abide by generally accepted museum standards, and otherwise act in accordance with the best interests of the institution and the public it serves. If there is even a hint that this is not the case, candidates may want to reconsider an application. Exceptions to cautionary advice are understandable if you are being hired to fix a problem, know it, and take a job offer with that assignment recognized. This is often the case for directors. As in the business world, all too often a new museum CEO is brought in to correct problems.

Government-Owned Museums

There are many government-owned and -operated museums in America. They can be found on the national, state, and local levels. Nationally, the most obvious example would be the Smithsonian Institution. On state levels, there are many state museums and historic sites. Locally, county and town museums abound. Hiring practices within government systems can be quite different from those implemented in the private sector. Working for government museums can be different also. Essentially a person is not working for a particular museum but for a government and an agency within that government. This skews reporting authority and supervisory capabilities. From a museum employee perspective, government jobs may be far more secure than ones found in the private sector. Additionally, benefits can be superior and also more secure.

Government-owned museums are not independent but are part of a larger operation. Working in them often requires using and relying on other government offices and departments. For instance, maintenance can be done by workers who fall outside the museum's immediate internal reporting structure. Unless there are emergencies, this means getting in line for plumbers, electricians, housekeeping, and other support operations. These folks may be well-trained and well-meaning, but their museum knowledge is limited. Similar considerations hold for security functions, bookkeeping, human relations, and retail sales.

Because there is minimal need for government museums to raise money outside of their official budgets, the customary pressure to focus on earned income and typical fundraising activities pursued by most museums is pretty much absent, or at least less prominent a necessity. There is a downside to the museum relying on government budgets, however. They must get in line with other agencies during designated budgeting processes to appeal for support from lawmakers. If there is an economic downturn which results in less tax revenue, museum budgets can suffer. Staff reductions are often a consequence.

Government museums may also welcome independent nonprofit ancillary support groups to raise additional funds not provided by government. Again, these are often referred to as the "Friends" of the particular museum. Because government museums are not nonprofit, tax-exempt entities, donations to them do not qualify for donor tax deductions. This is circumnavigated by the Friends groups, which are always organized as nonprofit entities. Dollar donations thus qualify as tax deductible.

From a job perspective, being a government employee or one working for a Friends group has its pros and cons. Candidates must understand both the financial and operating differences. Who decides what the Friends group does, when, how, and with whom? Who decides what fundraising will be done, when, and, how? Is the Friends group totally independent of the government museum? Will the Friends group have any influence over the operations of the museum?

Company Museums

Few museums are owned by companies, but the designation needs to be recognized. One prominent example is the Wells Fargo bank that collects artifacts of its history which dates back to 1852. Its website (http://www .wellsfargohistory.com) lists eleven museums located around the country. Corporate museums are subject to the whims of the business leadership. With no charitable nonprofit mission, they can do as they wish with collections, programs, staffing, etc. This does not make for very secure employment of museum professionals. Nevertheless, as is the case with Wells Fargo, some have survived for many years.

The Hard Rock company with its hotels, cafés, and casinos around the world may not be or have a museum per se, but in essence it operates a global museum enterprise when one considers the huge collection of rock and roll memorabilia it owns and displays at its many locations. Each has a unique collection theme. The employees have functions similar to those found in museums. It also hires companies and individuals who perform museum-like tasks on a contract basis.

Academic Museums: College or University

Academic museums are found throughout the nation. This is a common museum form. Many are art museums, although the University of Pennsylvania has long boasted one of the world's great museums of archaeology and anthropology. These museums are owned by colleges and universities. They are generally well-run and professionally staffed. Given the nature of their structure and support mechanisms, funding is relatively secure.

The drawback of most academic museums is caused by the nature of their ownership. What makes them relatively secure operations can also cause great harm. These are not independent operations governed by their own board of trustees. While they may have honorary boards, or committees, or support bodies, they are ultimately under the legal authority of the college or university that possesses them.

Most of the time academic museums tend to operate with little adverse interference from their governing department or office. Unfortunately, on occasion, huge controversies can erupt when decisions are proposed or made that undermine the purpose of a museum. Recently the most prominent of these have targeted museum collections, one unsuccessfully and one successfully. In 2009, Brandeis University board of trustees proposed closing its Rose Art Museum and selling the collections. The outcry was so vitriolic in 2011, that the proposal was dropped. In 2017, the board of trustees of La

Salle University in Philadelphia, PA, decided to sell forty works of art from its museum. In spite of loud opposition, the sale proceeded. Museum staff in neither museum was consulted about these sales. The proceeds were for the schools' general fund, not to benefit either museum.

The advantages and disadvantages of academic museum ownership need to be recognized by prospective employees. During the interview process, questions about authority, workload, oversight, and other practical matters need to be discussed. Academic museums can also have Friends groups. The nature, authority, influence, and structure of these should reflect the same concerns as those outlined for any museum.

Museum Facilities Owned by a Larger Entity

Job candidates will benefit from knowing if the museum where they are seeking a job does not own its own building but either rents or has been given space within a larger structure or organization. College and university museums often reflect this facility arrangement, but private museums may too. The Museo del Barrio is in a larger building owned by the City of New York. The La Salle University Art Museum is in the basement of a classroom building. The United States Naval Academy Museum is at the United States Naval Academy in Maryland.

Depending on the job being sought, applicants will want to know who makes facility decisions for such museums. Who owns the collections? Who sets personnel compensation and benefit decisions? What governing authority is in place for the museum, and does it have any actual authority? What sort of money can these museums raise and for what purpose?

The City of New York owns the property and sometimes the buildings of many museums around the five boroughs. While the individual museums may be their own legal entities with boards of trustees, etc., depending on a particular position, employees either work for the museum or the city. Regardless of this arrangement, it is not unusual for all employees to receive the same quality and quantity of benefits. (Fortunately, for the most part, the collections do not belong to the city and are thus protected from unwise potential or actual political assaults.) Programming is generally unencumbered by city influence. There is often a designated board member assigned by the mayor.

Only once in recent history has city funding of such a museum been threatened. This occurred when the Brooklyn Museum mounted an exhibition that contained a work of art offensive to Roman Catholics. The then mayor, a Catholic, threatened to withdraw the city's annual support unless the painting was removed. It was not. City funding continued, as it does to this day.

Nevertheless, employees of these museums need to be mindful of potential backlashes by cranky politicians.

LOCATION, LOCATION, LOCATION

Museums are found all over the place. As noted previously, cities have many. Suburban settings host more than a few. Small towns have them, mostly in the form of local historical societies or historic houses (often one and the same). And, they can be found in remote rural locations. Unlike sports stadia, or amusement parks, or casinos, though they might wish it, museums are often not easily reached by the general public.

When looking for a museum job, candidates should consider what locale is more or less appealing. What are the advantages and disadvantages of a particular place? Some parts of the United States are more expensive to live in than others. Some have easy access to major highways, airports, and public transportation. What sort of social life can one expect in various places and will it reflect your interests? If politics is important to you, will you be looking for work in a conservative or liberal area? What demographics are you comfortable with?

Will a job cause a museum professional to be typecast as a specialist in history, science, or art museums, or ancillary aspects of those kinds of organizations? Certain museum jobs, such as curating, tend to focus on particular academic and scholarly areas. Others, such as maintenance, hold more employment latitude.

Finally, when considering a museum's location, job applicants must also know if they will need to commute and how. Of the six museum jobs I have had, the longest commute was in New York City. It took thirty-five minutes by public transportation and walking. The shortest commute was a stroll from a house I rented on the property of a museum to my office. Other commutes were by car and easily done. It is not unusual for people to accept an hour or more commute for personal and economic reasons. In addition, some employees never relocate their home base and rent places near where they work so they can go home on weekends and holidays. This can be complicated. No one can be fired for not living in a certain place unless a geographical boundary is required for the job, if indeed such a restriction is legal.

Sometimes we have no choice about where we look for work. Family or other personal realities may have us living in a locale we cannot leave. This usually means finding a job nearby. How nearby depends, but within a reasonable commuting distance tends to be the norm. Five minutes to an hour is a customary range. Long-distance commuting happens, although it can wear on an individual and on personal relationships. These jobs are often far enough away to require overnight separations from loved ones.

From an employer's perspective, I am always cautious about staff who commute long distances. In spite of what they say or promise, there are always delays or absences for all sorts of reasons. Accommodating these can be done and may even be required if they are in accord with institutional policies. Museum job candidates should be aware that if they need to commute long distances, another, and closer, candidate may get the job. Furthermore, it should go without saying that a commute time should be mentioned by applicants during an interview.

RESEARCH THE MUSEUM

Learn as much as you can about the prospective museum and the person(s) you will be meeting with. The more you know, the better your interview will be.

Finally, before applying to any position, you will need to research the museum along with any institution it is affiliated with. Gathering this information brings all of the criteria mentioned in this chapter into focus. Following is a list of information sources that you should use to learn about the museum to which you are applying for a job. Gather as much information as you can before deciding to apply for the job; this information will be especially important to you in the interview process.

- Devour the website, every tab, every detail.
- Look up such publicly available official documentary materials as the museum's:
  - 990 tax filing
  - Bylaws
  - Articles of incorporation
- Seek online or hard copy:
  - Annual reports
  - Newsletters
  - Catalogues and other publications
  - Staff organization chart
  - Personnel manual
    - Performance review

- Legal requirements
- Expenditure approvals and reimbursements
- Personal work on the job
- Dress code
- Work at home
- Personal use of museum facilities and equipment
- Ownership of work products (e.g., catalogues, books, art)
- IT rules and regulations
- Work hours: on premises, off, virtually
- Harassment coverage, sexual, political, economic, trustee interference, illegal activities
- Whistle-blower protection
- Employee complaint procedures
- Benefits
  - Vacation
  - Medical
  - Retirement
  - Family leave
  - Holidays
  - Bereavement
  - Personal days
  - Professional advancement support
    - Sabbatical
    - Tenure
    - Research, writing, copyright or patent ownership, income derived therefrom
  - Conflict-of-interest forms, for trustees and staff
  - Code of ethics
  - Samples of media coverage
  - Annual audit
  - Annual budget
  - Recent board meeting minutes
  - Strategic or long-range plan
  - Various policies, such as collection policy
  - Annual calendar, of events, meetings
  - Attendance procedures
- Check online listings and media coverage not generated by the museum.
- Research staff and board of trustees: how many, names, backgrounds.
- If possible and you are comfortable doing so, talk with staff and/or trustees about the museum . . . and each other.
- Provided they are familiar with it, talk to colleagues about the institution.

- Visit the museum before your interview, when possible. Not letting on you are a job candidate is probably beneficial during the visit.
- Talk to people in the community about the museum.
- Talk to people you know in the field about the museum.
- Envision yourself in whatever sort of job appeals to you
- Try to see how a museum might envision you in a particular job.
- Some museum jobs are union jobs, learn if this is the case with the one you seek.
- Look up a museum's rating with companies that rate nonprofit entities. The most notable of these are: GuideStar (http://www.guidestar.org) and Charity Navigator (http://www.charitynavigator.org).

CONCLUSION

As a job candidate, deciding on the sort of museum one likes is both an intellectual and an intuitive exercise. When it comes to a museum subject, be it science, art, or history, individuals in the field tend to typecast early on. For that reason, a museum's size, location, ownership structure, or longevity may be less important than the particular work being sought. Opportunities can appear in a wide range of places. Exceptions to discipline conformity would be for jobs that can be done in any museum. These would certainly include maintenance, security, and finance positions.

In assessing the combination of museum profiles discussed in this chapter, employment preferences and conclusions will become evident, reinforced, or in some cases discovered. By the time a candidate has weighed all the options, he or she will be much more comfortable in making decisions. The more research employment candidates do, the better decisions they can make regarding their career. And, remember, the process of elimination is as important as the process of selection.

NOTES

    1. Steve Freiss, "In the Car Museum Race, Some Drop Out," *New York Times*, May 10, 2018, https://www.nytimes.com/2018/05/10/business/car-museums-closing.html.
    2. Daniel Strohl, "World's Largest Ford Museum to Close, May Sell Entire Collection at Once," *Hemmings Daily*, October 27, 2016, https://www.hemmings.com/blog/2016/10/27/worlds-largest-ford-museum-to-close-may-sell-entire-collection-at-once/.

Chapter Four

Job Listings

The more flexible you are in your museum job searches, the more employment options you have. Duh.

Museum job hunters have more options than they might realize. Traditionally, the first place to look for work was in hard copy classified ads as found in newspapers, magazines, and through museum membership organizations. Those continue to be relevant, but the Internet is the common employment conduit, especially since newspapers, professional newsletters, magazines, and the like are all available online. The job search sources listed in this chapter are easily found. Though the process can be time consuming, the time is well worth the effort. These can fluctuate, so be on the lookout for new options.

ONLINE EMPLOYMENT SOURCES

Most postings for jobs are now online, so this is where you will do most of your research. There are many specific sites to visit. Some of them are for museum jobs exclusively, while others handle all sorts of employment options. Several will post your résumé though usually for a small fee. Some of the more important sites are listed here. This list will change over time. Be watchful and stay current by asking friends and colleagues for advice and suggestions.

MUSEUM-SPECIFIC SITES

- American Alliance of Museums (AAM), "Find a Job" (AAM Job HQ), https://aam-us-jobs.careerwebsite.com/
- American Association for State and Local History (AASLH), "Career Center," https:/jobs.aaslh.org
- Association of Academic Museums and Galleries (AAMG), "Job Postings," https://www.aamg-us.org/wp/category/general-announcement/jobs/
- Association of Art Museum Directors (AAMD), "Current Opportunities," https://aamd.org/museum-careers/current-opportunities
- College Art Association of America, Inc., "Jobs & Opportunities," http://www.collegeart.org/jobs-and-opportunities
- Museum Employment Resource Center, "Job Vacancy Index," http://museum-employment.com/
- Museum Hack, "Jobs and Careers," https://museumhack.com/jobs/
- MuseumJobsOnline.com, http://museumjobsonline.com/MJO
- Museum Market, "Jobs," http://www.museummarket.com/Jobs.htm
- New York Foundation for the Arts, "NYFA Classifieds," https://www.nyfa.org/classifieds and "Job Listings," https://www.nyfa.org/jobs

Additionally, check

- Individual museum websites
- State or local museum associations

General/Related Job Sites

- ArtJobs, http://www.artjobs.com
- Indeed, http://www.indeed.com
- Federal job listings
- Jobmonkey, http://www.jobmonkey.com
- LinkedIn, "Jobs," https://www.linkedin.com/jobs
- USA Jobs, www.usajobs.gov
- ZipRecruiter, http://www.ziprecruiter.com

Search Firms

As with most professions, there are search firms that include museum jobs. Here are just a few that work with museums.

- Arts Consulting Group, http://artsconsulting.com/
- Management Consultants for the Arts, https://www.mcaonline.us/

- Museum Management Consultants, Inc., http://museum-management.com/
- m/Oppenheim, https://www.moppenheim.com/
- Opportunity Resources, Inc, https://www.opportunityresources.net/
- Russell Reynolds Associates, http://www.russellreynolds.com/

INFORMAL EMPLOYMENT SOURCES

Informal employment inquiries follow the usual pattern for any profession. Because employment situations ebb and flow, opportunities are always in flux. When chatting with the sorts of contacts listed below, be prepared to supply your résumé.

- School alumni/ae
- Friends
- Connections
- Colleagues in related fields
- Cold calls: independent approach by phone, email, or letter, to the director or someone in authority
- Museum professionals: ask for jobs or advice
- Newspapers and arts, history, science, or museum journals

In thinking about a job, consider not only the job itself but where it can take you professionally. What will you learn and how will that impact your résumé? Ask yourself what the next job would be after you secure the job you are considering. But do not reject the idea that a particular job might be the ideal one for you for a very long time!

FULL-TIME MUSEUM JOBS

As you sort through job advertisements (online, in print, or via informal sources), you will find that there are essentially three types of full-time museum jobs. Each offers different opportunities. Some questions will help you to determine whether to apply for the position.

- New job
- Existing job
- Reconfigured job

New Jobs

New jobs can be exciting, precarious, or a bit of both. Candidates must ask exactly what will be expected of the position. The following questions will help:

- Why has it been created?
- Is it experimental?
- How is it being funded?
- Whom does the employee report to, how, and when?
- What resources will the employee have and are these new also, or, what is already available at the work place?
- How will the success or failure of the job be assessed, by whom, and when?
- How much independence will the employee have regarding the work to be done?
- Will the employee have any input regarding the nature of the job as it unfolds over time?
- How is the position perceived within the overall museum, especially with other staff, and more especially with the person's immediate supervisor?
- Is there any trustee or other volunteer involvement with the job?

Existing Jobs

Existing jobs have a track record and can presumably be well explained and understood by job applicants. Some of the same questions to ask about a new job apply and are listed here; others are listed in chapter 7.

- Why is the job open?
- If the person who had it before is available, may I talk to him or her?
- Is the salary and benefit package the same as it was previously, and if not, may I ask about the change?
- How is the position funded, within the annual budget?
- Will the employee be invited to submit ideas regarding changing the position once hired and on the job for a while?

Reconfigured Jobs

Reconfigured jobs are ones that retain certain duties and responsibilities of an earlier job, while some duties and responsibilities have been eliminated or adjusted, new ones have been added to meet changing institutional needs. The same sorts of questions listed above and in chapter 7 need to be asked. Additional questions should include:

- Why was the job changed?
- How has the change been greeted by board and staff?
- Is there a chance that the job will revert to its former profile?
- Can the new employee suggest further changes once hired?
- Is this an experimental change that might make the job subject to elimination if it is deemed untenable?

Part-Time Museum Jobs

As noted in the preface, this volume does not focus on part-time, seasonal, hourly, temporary, or contract work. While application processes can be similar to those discussed herein, long-term secure employment prospects either fall outside the nature of such jobs or are often negligible. Getting a "foot in the door" can be a desirable strategic maneuver, but desired museum full-time employment may be wishful thinking.

THE JOB AD

Typical museum job ads can be brief. They list a job title, reporting structure, and work schedule, along with the responsibilities as well as academic credentials and experience desired. The more one delves into a particular job application, often the more detailed a museum's description and expectations will be. Do your homework. Feel free to ask questions early in the process. Assess the museum's employment expectations in the context of the museum's work environment and record. Does the job description make sense? Does it align with what the museum says it wants? Will it provide the resources to effectively accomplish its needs and objectives?

Museums often note they are "equal opportunity" employers. This is a positive hiring announcement. Applicants can ask for definitions if they wish, but it is generally understood to guard against gender, race, ethnicity, age, domestic status, religion, and related personal profiles. If the fact is not listed in a job ad or in the application material, applicants may want to ask why.

Beware of the generic line found toward the end of many job descriptions: ". . . and other duties as assigned." This means you can be told to do all sorts of things regardless of how they correspond with what you were hired to do. This might happen rarely, if at all, but it can lead to distracting from your main purpose and focus. If you can get it removed from a job description, that is helpful.

Museum hiring often takes longer than anticipated for either the museum or a candidate. Patience is a virtue.

CONCLUSION

Employment notices vary widely in the museum field. They can be simple personnel announcements posted on an institution's website or unfold conversationally between and among museum staff and trustees. Highly professional museums will follow a more customary and formal path. They will not only post jobs on their websites but on customarily viewed sites organized by museum profession organizations. Job seekers are advised to consider all options, including self-motivated direct inquiries. It is important to monitor the changing nature of museum employment both insofar as job descriptions are concerned, and where and how job openings are made known within the profession.

Chapter Five

The Job Application

APPLYING FOR A JOB

There are several ways to apply for a museum job. You may initiate an inquiry yourself. More often you will respond to posted employment notices. Occasionally you will answer personal or written requests to be a candidate. And, positions may open as a natural consequence of vacancies caused by retirement, death, or other forms of a vacancy requiring hiring.

Customary ways of learning about a museum job are noted in chapter 4. To proceed with an application, you should follow the instructions listed in an employment notice, unless you are initiating an inquiry on your own and no application announcement or process has been made.

When you are responding to an employment notice or a personal request from a museum, *FOLLOW THE INSTRUCTIONS* in the notice or those given you by the personal contact. This is not the time to be cutely creative. Here are some tips to follow (unless directed otherwise by the instructions in the job ad).

- When a letter of application is requested, write one. The recommended length is one page. Two or even three is acceptable depending on what you want to say and how. The letter lets your personality show through in a way a résumé does not.
- If references are requested, give the required number. Make sure they are appropriate for the job you seek. Your old scoutmaster may know your personal qualities from when you were fourteen, but he or she probably cannot really comment on your work experience or professional dedication. Be certain you have prior approval from your references to list their names.

- Do not use a generic reference letter or email, or one not addressed to a person at the interviewing museum for a specific job. "To Whom It May Concern" is an unacceptable salutation. If there is no individual to address, the reference can be for a specific position and you can write, after the name and address of the museum, "RE: Job Title . . ."
- If salary expectations are requested, include them. You can give a range, or say what you are making now (and you would like to improve that), or give a specific number. You can also equivocate by mentioning the influence the value of benefits would have on your expectations. Remember, benefits can amount from 10 to 30 percent of compensation.
- Should you be asked if the museum can contact your current employer respond, "Yes" or "No." Either is fine, though "No" is usually preferred by an applicant. This will be understood by a prospective employer because applicants often do not want their current employer to know they are looking for another job.
- If asked about when you are available if hired, give them a time frame. It is perfectly acceptable to say a few weeks at least, so as to give your current employer fair notice. This shows a professional attitude.
- If you apply for a job and do not hear back from the museum, follow up.
  - Be careful how you do this so as to avoid annoying the museum.
  - Timing may be important, and you may want to wait longer than you might wish.

Don't ruffle job application feathers needlessly. There can be many mistakes made or difficulties encountered when seeking employment. Fortunately, most processes go smoothly, but you are at the mercy of the employer.

THE APPLICATION LETTER

Job application letters offer wonderful opportunities to let your voice be heard in ways a résumé cannot. While the recommended length is one page, two is permissible depending on the job being sought. Though generally frowned upon, three is sometimes acceptable. There are online sites recommending how to write an application letter. These are fine but remember, none really address museums and museum jobs. Nevertheless, it will do no harm to review some.

A few recommendations can be made.

- Unless otherwise stated in a job announcement or instructed elsewhere, always address the letter to an individual. Most museums are small enough to know who these recipients might be. Call the museum for advice. If a "cc" is suggested, be certain those recipients are appropriate.

- Keep personal stories, anecdotes, and humor to a minimum, if at all. This is a job search rather than a social exercise.
- Avoid solo acronyms such as AAM, or AASLH, or MAAM. While these are for organizations within the museum field, and may be known by the recipient, they may not recognize them and they look odd in a letter (American Alliance of Museums, The American Association for State and Local History, the Middle Atlantic Association of Museums).
- Have someone outside the museum world proof your letter.
- Have someone inside the museum world proof your letter.

THE RÉSUMÉ

There are scads of online sites about writing résumés. Most of the advice is either obvious or inapplicable to museum work. You can sort that out easily. The vast majority of the sites discuss looking for work in the corporate commercial business world. While the goal of getting a job is the same as in the nonprofit sector, how to do so in that sector requires a different mindset. There are online references and books about writing résumés. These sources have valued information, but some of it may not pertain to seeking a job in a museum. Skills and abilities are important, but attitude and devotion to a cause is of equal value.

One thing that stands out when reading about job searches in the corporate world is the amount of time a résumé is said to be looked at upon receipt. It is short. For the most part, that is not true in museum circles. A résumé may be tossed aside, misread, or read by the wrong people, but a cursory glance is usually not the rule. In my experience, even when not seeking an employee, unsolicited résumés are read. Some are even kept should an opening occur for which a person seems qualified.

Always keep your résumé current (but not voluminous; one page is usually sufficient), whether or not you are looking for work.

You have to decide how to present your work history in a clear, pertinent, and succinctly informative manner. It is advisable to have an outside source critique your résumé. Avoid family and friends or even work colleagues who know you. An independent appraisal, even if from someone unfamiliar with museum work, will probably provide a more unbiased opinion.

Be prepared to adjust your résumé for a particular job search. This does not mean lying or being coy. It means emphasizing aspects of your career that are more relevant or of more value to a particular application than other parts of your experience. Always have an up-to-date résumé. On the job, be sure the résumé in your personnel file is current.

It is usually of the utmost importance to keep your job searches confidential. How you define confidential is up to you. If you are employed, your employer and co-workers will probably not be told about your search for another job. Some family and friends need not know either. Those at a museum where you are seeking work can be similarly kept out of the loop or have their confidentiality requested.

The form and format of your résumé is yours to decide upon. You can use outlines suggested in online sites, write a narrative version, or make some combination of both. The goal is to provide an accurate, current overview of your work while not dwelling at length on details. As an example, the author's one-page résumé is provided on the next page.

Tips for what to include in your résumé are as follows:

- Obvious—your name, mailing address, and contact information such as email address, preferred phone number, etc. should be included, usually at the top.
- Social media.
  - Control your social media presence to avoid contradictory profiles or information that will work against your career advancement, be it on Instagram, LinkedIn, YouTube, Twitter, Pinterest, Facebook, a personal website, etc. Potential employers will look at all of these. Clean them up if necessary, before you apply for any job.
- Make sure a phone number(s) is one you will actually answer.
  - If it is where you currently work, be sure you can talk privately and in confidence.
  - If a message is left, respond quickly.
  - If you have to leave a message, sound upbeat, enthusiastic, and clear; make the message succinct and to the point; and leave the number where you prefer to be reached.
- Make sure you use the email address where you want to be contacted. Usually this is a personal address. If your current work email address is private and only you will see it, that may be included.
- List jobs in chronological order with the current or most recent one first. Unless specifically requested by a museum, include the year you started and the year you left a particular job. For your current job, the year you started followed by a hyphen and the word "Present" is customary. You

Author's Sample One Page Résumé

Preferred Name, Address, Phone, Email, and, Website if relevant. Social media contacts optional.

2013 – 2018	Executive Director, Boscobel Restoration, Inc., Garrison, NY
2010 – 2013	Museum Consultant, Writer, Educator, Trustee
2010 – 2011	Currier & Ives Print Collection Project, Museum of the City of New York
2010 – Present	Executive Director Emeritus, Morris Museum, Morristown, NJ
2001-2010	Executive Director, Morris Museum and the Bickford Theatre, Morristown, New Jersey, Executive Vice President, Morris Museum Foundation
1995-2001	Executive Director, Bennington Museum, Bennington, Vermont
1991-1995	Director of Museums, Western Reserve Historical Society, Cleveland, Ohio
1987-1991	Assistant Director, Maine State Museum, Augusta, Maine
1985-1987	Senior Curator, Museum of the City of New York, (MCNY) NYC
1979-1985	Department Head/Curator: Paintings, Prints, Photographs, MCNY
1977-1979	Curator of Prints and Photographs, MCNY
1973-1977	Assistant Curator, Paintings, Prints and Photographs, MCNY
1971-1972	Assistant to the Senior Curator, MCNY

Member, Century Association, NYC

Art Committee, Park Avenue Club, Florham Park, NJ

Board of Governors: Bard - St. Stephens Alumni/ae Association

American Alliance of Museums, Accreditation Visiting Committee

Collections Committee, Fraunces Tavern Museum, New York, NY

Visiting Scholar, American Academy in Rome, 2017

Teaching

Seton Hall University, Adjunct Professor, Museum Studies, 2002 – Present

New York University, School of Continuing and Professional Studies, Adjunct Professor, 2010

Case Western Reserve University, Adjunct Professor, Museum Studies, 1991-94

New York University, NYC, Graduate Program in Archival Management and Historical Editing, Lecturer, 1978-87

New York University School of Continuing Education, Lecturer, 1986-88

The New School for Social Research, NY: Center for New York City Affairs, Adjunct Professor, 1978, 1984

Columbia University, NY, New York, the Graduate School of Architecture and Planning, New York Neighborhood Seminar, Lecturer, 1981-82

Education

B.A., Bard College, Sculpture, Annandale-on-Hudson, NY

International Graduate Certificate, Principles of Conservation Science, (UNESCO) International Centre for the Study of the Preservation and Restoration of Cultural Property, Rome, Italy can include a sentence or two about what the job is and what you accomplished of note.

- Employers like consistency and logic in résumés. If there are questionable gaps between jobs, or if you had a lot of jobs over a short period of time, you will need to explain this either in the letter of application, interview, or both.
- For people seeking their first job, internships, years at school, summer jobs, etc. will be acceptable. As your career advances these can be reduced and even eliminated.
- Some résumé models have the category of Objective at the start. Forget this. Your objective is obviously to get the particular job you are seeking. Personal interests may be interesting to you and others, but they really don't need to be on a résumé. Who cares if you like cats, archery, yodeling, or taking long walks on the beach. This sort of stuff can be mentioned in interviews if appropriate.
- In addition to jobs, you might want to list exhibits you've done or programs for which you are or have been responsible, collection duties, talks you gave, publications you have written, and any consulting work.
- Veterans may wish to list this fact, including service branch, rank upon discharge, awards, and dates of enlistment.
- You need not list your GPA either for college or graduate school. Unless you think they are important to note, you may leave out the organizations you belonged to in the past.
- Awards can be included, but they should be relevant and significant (not something you got in the eighth grade for perfect attendance).
- Certifications, computer or mechanical skills, and languages can be listed if you think they enhance your résumé or are otherwise significant and relevant to the job you seek.
- The longer you are in a profession, usually, the longer your résumé will be, but always have a one-page version. These are not applicable when seeking a job and interviewing but for providing information in a succinct form when requested.
- Listing professional organizations that you are associated with can be informative.

"Never, ever describe yourself as 'innovative,' 'energetic,' 'a team player,' 'a self-starter,' or a 'good communicator.' These words and terms are so overused they have become meaningless."[1]

1. Gary Burnison, *Lose the Resume, Land the Job*, (Hoboken, NJ: John Wiley & Sons, Inc., 2018), 121.

REFERENCES

Good references are critical to a successful job hunt. The museum world remains small enough to cause employers to rely significantly on personal, professional opinions about candidates. In selecting references, be certain they are more than willing to be supportive, know your abilities, achievements, and personality. Be sure they will be comfortable being contacted directly by a prospective employer. While you will want to avoid the jargon below, your references may embrace such words if they are reliable descriptions of you and your work.

SELECTING REFERENCES

- Select appropriate references for the specific job you are seeking, not generic ones who once offered to help whenever needed.
- Select references who can speak about you and your current or recent work as it relates to the job you are applying for.
- Do not use irrelevant people, such as your married lover (I'm not kidding).
- Make sure your references have agreed to be a reference for the specific job you are seeking.
- Make sure reference names, titles, and contact information are current and correct.
- Ask your references to let you know if they are contacted and what is said.
- Do not simply keep a standard list of references that you use whenever applying for a job.
- Avoid generic reference letters. The contact between your prospective employer and a reference should be personal and direct without your involvement.
- Be certain you give the exact number of references requested.
- Be prepared to submit more references if asked.
- Ask your references to refrain from mentioning other jobs you may be seeking when they are contacted for a specific position.
- If there is a chance your references will be contacted more than once, as would be the case when you are applying for more than one job, make sure this is acceptable to them before listing them in an application.

BEING REQUESTED TO APPLY FOR A JOB

What if an influential person or persons contact you about a job out of the blue? Similarly, how do you respond if you are approached by influential people at the museum where you currently work to apply for another job at that museum? In both cases, you thank the people profusely for their support of you. Assess where you are in your personal life and career. Decide if the job is of interest and if you would be able to do it. Consider the outcomes if you decline versus if you apply.

In the case of the recommendation about a job at another museum, your involvement will be less potentially prickly than for the one where you are already working. You can easily decline the other museum job if you wish and presumably there will be no adverse fallout. The same may be true for the one at the museum where you work. However, if you do apply for that job and don't get it, there can be undue consequences.

Advancement within a museum can have very different characteristics than those of applying for a job outside a museum where you already are. With the latter, you seek or are asked to apply and that can be quite a confidential process unknown to your current museum. In fact, usually few, if any, know you are interested in leaving where you are until you announce your departure.

There can be two distinct approaches to seeking another job where you work. The change may be obvious, inevitable, ideal for you, and embraced by all, so that the museum has no interest in opening the post to other candidates. Or, other candidates, internal and external, may be encouraged to apply. In the latter case, you will presumably be part of a pool of finalists. Remember though—you may have been given this status only as a courtesy to your current employment. With internal scenarios, five outcomes can unfold.

- The museum staff will be satisfied with the result.
- The museum staff will be unsatisfied with the result.
- If you are selected you will presumably be delighted.
- If you are selected, competing internal candidates may hold a grudge, as might their supporters.
- If you are not selected, do not project anger, disappointment, upset, or other adverse emotions on the job, and do not let supporters you may have had do the same.

How a museum considers internal applicants for a job will vary from institution to institution. Larger museums usually follow customary hiring processes. Smaller museums may be much less formal. Occasionally, decisions are based on favoritism at the loss of a better candidate.

Because most museums are small and have limited human resource capabilities, they can stumble when it comes to generally accepted hiring customs or laws about the process.

CONCLUSION

Applying for any job is both a science and an art. Museum employment is not exempt from this reality. All the credentials in the world cannot overcome weak written presentations. Conversely, attention-getting writing cannot cover for an empty résumé. When seeking a museum position, consider how qualified you are for it and do your best to make that clear in the materials submitted. Have a third party review your application. A third party can be someone from within the museum field as well as someone unfamiliar with it. There are times when specialists use such obscure language that even the most experienced reader is confused. Most of us are nervous when discussing ourselves as we apply for a job. This is especially true early in careers. Conversely, we want to avoid being overly boastful or self-congratulatory. A middle ground is the best place to be. Good luck!

Chapter Six

The Museum Interviews You

If your job application is favorably considered, an interview will usually be scheduled. Congratulations. This is a—*if not THE*—critical face-to-face step in applying for work of any sort. Job interviews are encounters in wishful thinking. The applicant wishes to get the job. The employer wishes to find the ideal employee. Interview skills are important. Prepare. Prepare. Prepare. Practice. Practice. Practice.

The following advice will provide an overview of what to expect or request as you plan for the interview and as it unfolds in reality. No detail is too small to ignore, but always keep the big picture in mind too. Some of what is contained here may never be mentioned during an interview, and there may be some surprises also. The key is to remain cool, calm, and collected while also being genuinely excited and enthusiastic about the prospect of working for a particular museum in a particular position. The Internet has various online interview sites, some wise, some foolish. Take a look and decide what is helpful. Remember, you are seeking to work in a museum, not some corporate office.

INTERVIEW LOGISTICS

Seeking work is the most important personal professional sales venture you will engage in. The language you use, your appearance, your sincerity, and your commitment to the field will be your most important assets when meeting with a prospective employer. You are not looking for work; you are pursuing a calling.

The employer will generally set interview time parameters for candidates. These include when and where to meet, and for how long, as well as when a candidate can expect to get responses after an interview.

Interview logistics include scheduling, travel, and cost. Most interviews are conducted in person, but some may be via Skype if distance is a factor. In this latter case, make sure you are technologically prepared for it. Test your equipment beforehand. Block out background interference. Turn off your cell phone and sound systems, and make sure you are in a room where you can't be interrupted by noises from family and pets.

Museums rarely pay for candidates' interview travel expenses, be they local or long distance. An exception is with director jobs.

Schedule the interview(s) to your advantage (when your "biorhythms" are at their best) if you can, but otherwise it's up to the employer. People understand if you have prior commitments, and some dates for travel time, holidays, etc., need to be factored into planning.

Depending on where the interview will occur and when, you may want to check the weather to avoid transit difficulties. There happened to be winter snowstorms when I had two different interviews (a month apart) for a director job. I made both. The board was impressed. While it was not the reason I was hired, it certainly looked good. My drive to the interview was an hour and a quarter one way.

Unless you are interviewing for your first job, an applicant usually tries to arrange a meeting unbeknownst to a current employer. Therefore, keep the process as confidential as possible. Take personal time off for meetings. You have no obligation to tell anyone at your place of work why you will be out that day or days (if traveling long distance). When applying for several jobs, you will need to judiciously juggle your times off to avoid suspicion.

If you accept a job at another museum, your current employer deserves the courtesy of being quickly informed about your departure. You should be aware of, and prepare for, any transition preparations before you leave. A smooth change of staff will contribute to your professional reputation. You should always be welcome at any museum you have left.

There will be occasions when you and your employer know you are looking for another job. This might be the case when a partner or spouse relocates, health dictates a change of locale, or for other personal or family reasons. It can also happen if your job is being eliminated or if everyone understands you are seeking to advance your career and have gone as far as you can where you are. Sometimes there is a mutually agreed upon reason between you and management for you to depart the museum where you are. I have only fired two people in my career, but have "moved a few others along" both for the good of the museum and themselves.

FIRST (AND POSSIBLY ONLY) INTERVIEW:
INTERVIEW BASICS

So, you have been invited for a job interview. This might be your first, and possibly only, interview for the job. Depending on the level of the job for which you applied, employers may interview a candidate only once; for higher-level jobs, there might be a second or even third interview. No matter, though, you need to approach every interview as if the job is the most important thing in your life—you need to be focused, prepared, and flexible. Following are some interview basics:

- Show up on time and at the right place!
- If possible, know who you will be meeting with and learn about them beforehand.
  ○ Interviewers may change at the last minute.
  ○ You may be interviewed by more than one person.
  ○ In addition to a staff person(s) interviewing you, a trustee(s) may be present.
- Bring whatever material you might have been requested to bring.
- Consider taking ancillary materials to illustrate your work, or send this along afterward if you think you are, and will continue to be, a viable candidate. (First ask if you can send in such material.)
- Dress appropriately: no cleavage for either men or women.
- The extent and nature of acceptable obvious physical appearances, including but not limited to piercings, tattoos, or hair treatments, will depend on the sort of job and what you think the museum (or person interviewing you) will tolerate.
- Dress to appear professional, competent, and capable.
- Poise: Some of the basics: Stand and sit up straight (and still). Look people in the eye. Speak clearly, not too fast, and don't mumble. Have a firm handshake. Smile. Don't scratch, sniff, cough, or sneeze. If you use a restroom before or at some point in an interview process, make sure your clothing is back in shape and your hands are dry when you exit the bathroom.
- Turn your cell phone off.
- If you have a meal during an interview, attend to your manners (do not chew with your mouth open; do not talk with your mouth full; know how to properly use a knife, fork, and napkin). Avoid sloppy foods such as French onion soup. Avoid food that requires eating with your hands if you can (sandwiches can be really messy). If alcohol is served, don't get drunk. There can be many pitfalls when eating with others, and these are just a few little recommendations.

- Take a copy of the résumé you submitted with the job application. An updated one is fine if there is an appreciable change, but point this out.
- Be prepared to meet with more than one person and in more than one place.
- Make sure your presence on/in any social network site will not embarrass you.
- Don't be afraid to say you don't know something in response to a question.
- Ask appropriate questions (see chapter 7).
- Don't be a suck-up.
- Remember, this will probably be the first face-to-face opportunity to convey what you know and why your background and personality would make you an excellent hire.
- Be prepared to encounter situations that you may find offensive or otherwise convince you the job is not of interest. In that case, politely and quietly withdraw as a candidate. If you are working with a search firm, presumably you can confidentially explain to them why you made your decision.

QUESTIONS EMPLOYERS MIGHT ASK

There are many questions that a prospective employer might ask during an interview. You should be prepared to answer a wide variety of questions—some of which you can anticipate, and some which might surprise you. If being interviewed by multiple individuals, you might be asked the same question by each person. Be prepared to respond to each (don't look bored; don't say you've already responded to that question). In no particular order, these are a few customary questions you might expect to be asked.

Question: Why do you want this job?

This should be the most important question a job applicant is asked. It should infuse every aspect of an interview.

On the surface, the answer to this question would seem to be: "I want the job because it is exactly what I love doing in museums and I think I am ideally suited and trained for it," or something along those lines. In reality, the interviewers will want more than a canned response. They will, or should, drill down asking all sorts of questions about your interest in a position and what you feel about the museum's mission and purpose.

Expressing enthusiasm, keen interest, and being able to explain your credentials for a job are how to answer this question. Be careful not to overapplaud yourself. Conversely, avoid underselling yourself. Be honest about your skills, abilities, accomplishments, and where you have come up short if that is relevant. For example, I have had a lot of experience in every aspect of museum operations except finance. Accounting and bookkeeping are absent in my résumé. I understand spreadsheets, budgets, and fiscal reports and have always relied on excellent staff in these areas. In interviews for director jobs, I have been frank about this. It has never been a stumbling block to being hired.

Avoid appearing too eager or being a sycophant when answering the question about why you want a particular job. These personality traits can work against job applicants. On the flip side, don't be flip when meeting. Avoid being critical, cynical, or condescending about the museum you hope employs you. Certainly, you may have ideas regarding how operations, programs, activities, public relations, events, exhibits, maintenance, or security could be improved or changed. There is no need to hide these during interviews, and, in fact, they may be well received. As with so many other interpersonal encounters in life, how something is said is often more important than what is said.

For example, never say you want this job because "I need a job!" "I have to get away from my current job!" "I can't find anything else now, so this will do for the time being." "I can't move and this is the only job available hereabouts at this time." Even intimating these responses will scuttle your chances of success. No one wants to hire someone who is only interested in getting away from where he or she is, or is stuck in some untenable personal circumstance. There might be circumstances along these lines that are contributing to your search for a new job, but at an interview, keep mum. Do remember though, the museum world is still small and people can investigate individual's motives for moving.

Question: Tell us about your professional background and qualifications.

This is a relatively easy question to respond to if you are comfortable that your background and qualifications are appropriate for the job you seek. Presumably the conversation will reflect your résumé and letter of application, which, presumably, everyone interviewing you has seen (and has with them at the interview). This is the part of a meeting where you can elucidate, elaborate, and expand upon your résumé and letter; it can and should be the meat of a meeting.

When hiring, museums seek qualified applicants. This may seem so obvious it should go without saying. By the time an interview is arranged, those representing the museum will have reviewed an applicant's résumé, letter of application, and any ancillary materials provided or sought. The interview should amplify and focus on your abilities, skills, track record, and most importantly, your potential to do the job superbly for the museum. The conversation will (should) be the same whether you are an outside candidate for a job or an inside one.

Stick to facts and figures if they are relevant. Watch the responses of those you are talking to. Listen and respond to their questions, comments, and observations. You will learn more about a museum's understanding of, and expectations for, a job at an interview than in any other way.

Don't be an egotistical show-off. I have had to learn to stop being pedantic. Others may not find me or my work as fascinating as I do. Job interviews are no place for "mansplaining."

Because interviews can be shorter than one might prefer, you may be asked to *briefly* provide examples of your work at the meeting. You may also be asked to supply materials after a meeting. It is difficult to carry a portfolio of accomplishments. Samples, though, might be in order. But do not haul mounds of stuff out of a rolling briefcase or portfolio unless asked at the time for specific items.

Discuss what you believe you will bring to a job that will be of value and importance, insofar as you understand the job. You will probably not know what other candidates are seeking the position. You can nevertheless offer a profile that will differentiate you from the competition and in an appealing manner.

Question: Tell us about your academic training and how it will be important or helpful for the job you seek here.

Most museum jobs require or call for a particular sort of academic background. For some, there are predetermined scholarly expectations, as would be the case with curators and conservators. Maintenance and security personnel may be exempt from a complex and lengthy formal education. However, these positions always benefit from classes, workshops, internships, etc. relevant to their fields. Participation in such activities is personally and professionally beneficial. It also looks good on a résumé and is well received in an interview.

How you answer the question will depend on your preferences, interests, and experiences. Some candidates have impressive and lengthy academic credentials. Others are more limited. I have no graduate degrees. This is unheard of for museum directors and curators today. It is also rare in mid-level management jobs. The idea of the brilliant autodidact is cute in the abstract, but except for certain hands-on jobs those sorts of applicants do not get far in the museum world these days.

Special disciplines within museums have graduate programs in their fields. These include conservation, curating, exhibit design, media relations, education, and financial management. People selected to be interviewed for jobs in these areas will no doubt have requisite education credentials.

How you present your academic training will depend on how you wish to define yourself and on the job you seek. Some education backgrounds can be immediate and obviously relevant. Others can be more obscure and even philosophical. You need to make sure you answer the question in ways those in the room immediately understand and accept as logical.

The longer one is in museum work, the less prominent academic credentials may become. When starting your career, they are of primary concern. As a résumé expands, conversations about one's schooling grow shorter.

Question: Tell us a little about yourself.

This is a question asked for three reasons: to lighten a conversation and let interviewers get a sense of a candidate; to allow candidates to tell things about themselves that are either illegal or uncomfortable to ask about; and to provide information that might be of interpersonal value for the candidate.

I have responded with a description of my domestic background and family life (including the fact that my children are adopted Koreans—definitely an off-limits interview question). I might also add that I play washboard in a jug band and am an amateur artist on occasion.

How to respond to this question and for how long is up to the candidate but don't let it divert the main purpose of an interview and take up too much time.

Question: What sort of supervisory experience do you have?

While on the surface this may seem solely directed at jobs that involve managing staff all the time, many jobs can involve managing people on a contract, part-time, or hourly basis. The details of supervising people are rarely listed at length in résumés. This question gives interviewers the opportunity to discuss a candidate's management experience, interests, and capabilities. Questions relating to this one will be: Who did you supervise, why, and for how long? Did you have to hire, monitor, and dismiss people? Could we talk to someone who reported to you? How successful were you within your organization in this regard? Who assigned and monitored your supervisory work?

If you have not had any supervisory experience, the question might be easy to answer. However, you may want to mention being interested in doing such work. Also, the museum may anticipate the job expanding to involve supervising people.

Question: Why are you in the museum field?

The answer to this question will vary from candidate to candidate. Presumably you are in the field because it has meaning for you, you think you contribute to some aspect of it, and you have a belief it has value for altruistic reasons that go beyond a paycheck. Obviously, museums do not provide essential services such as hospitals, homeless shelters, schools, or fire departments do. But, they fulfill valued functions, and your work in and with museums is meaningful for you for reasons you can explain in an interview.

Question: What would you describe as your employment strengths?

Museums want employees who are smart, good at their jobs, and work well in a productive manner with others. It will be important to touch on these characteristics as you answer this question. Presumably your references will be able to confirm your strengths. There are many ways to respond, and you need to decide what is best for you in consideration of the job you seek and the people with whom you are interviewing.

Question: What would you describe as your employment weaknesses?

I have never encountered this question during the many interviews I have been involved with. However, it is always listed as something to be able to respond to when meeting with a potential employer. The advice is to allude to a strength as a weakness. For example, "I can get so involved in my work I need to schedule down time." Or, "I need to understand that those I am working with may not share my enthusiasm for a particular subject that totally absorbs me." As noted earlier, I always explain that I have no skills as a bookkeeper or accountant and therefore need people who can do this well.

Question: Veterans may be asked about their service.

You may respond as you think best. But, you may want to avoid lengthy conversations regarding opinions about the military and any engagements you or it are or were involved in. Occasionally veterans are given preferred hiring status. This can obviously work to an applicant's advantage and should not be declined or ignored. Depending on the nature of one's service, skills acquired during this time can be of value to a museum. Do not be shy about explaining what you did and how that would benefit an institution.

Question: What skills do you think you'd bring to this job?

Specific jobs usually have specific requirements for how they should be done, when, where, and by whom. Job descriptions will list these, but applicants must investigate in more detail what is expected. In the realm of public relations, knowing how to promote a museum is essential. Promoting a museum may not be the same as promoting a hospital, company, school, library, etc. Candidates for this sort of job need to know audience development, the language of the field, and how and where information should be posted. While hard copy media outlets are said to be less prevalent, they remain important for museums, along with virtual media options.

Your answers to this question may not be the ones expected (which can be said for most interview inquiries). Many people in museum work are only vaguely aware of what colleagues do, how, or why. This is especially true for trustees. If your responses are met with blank stares, or if you are asked totally irrelevant questions, you have an education task on hand. It is hard to do in the midst of an interview as you may or may not have the time. Moreover, you don't want to insult or annoy the questioner.

Question: Do you have any questions about the job?

This is a good question and often considered important. A few good responses will impress an interview group. This is more fully described in chapter 7, "You Interview the Museum."

Question: Could you give us an example of a failed project or assignment and why it happened and how you dealt with it?

This is one of those interview questions considered standard for any job application. I have never asked it or been asked. Nevertheless, be prepared for it, but be careful. Choose an example that does not suggest you are blaming anyone, or one organization, but a situation. You may want to avoid suggesting the failure was totally your fault. Again, situations may fail for many reasons. A sense of humor may be helpful when answering this, as you point a finger at yourself in the context of something larger.

Question: Tell us about your interpersonal skills.

Because museums are collaborative ventures, most jobs involve people working with people. As an example, an exception would be the midnight to 8 a.m. security watch at Boscobel Restoration in Garrison, NY. It is a post held by one person who never interacts with the public or other staff. Otherwise, museum employees need to have the ability to work productively with other staff but also members of the public, trustees, consultants, contract workers, volunteers, etc.

You can easily explain that, in your opinion, your interpersonal skills are excellent. You may be asked to give an example. Or you may want to offer an example or two.

Question: Will you be able to meet the schedule required of the job?

It is important to know exactly what a work schedule is or might be and what sort of variances could occur. I hired a person to head a museum's buildings and grounds department, and after a few months realized he would not work on weekends or evenings. He discovered he could do this because other maintenance staff filled in. It severely compromised scheduling options and caused other staff to think he enjoyed some privileged employment status. (The fact that he was married but had a "close personal relationship" with another staff person in authority, who was also married, only encouraged his deviousness.)

People have lives beyond those of their jobs. Of course, not everyone can work every time a museum may need them, but it is important when hiring to be sure you understand what is usually expected of you. Once that is clear, you can answer this question. Naturally, when interviewed, the unfortunate example I cited above said he could work most whenever he was needed. This schedule requirement was contained in his job description. Lying is something to avoid when interviewing.

Question: What do you see as the various roles technology plays in this job?

The world is awash with technology of all sorts, and museum jobs have their fair share. Most of what we think of relates to information technology, meaning computers and the like. But it also involves machinery, tools, equipment, and vehicles. Few (no?) museum positions are exempt from technology knowledge requirements. Job candidates will either be asked to explain their computer or other skills or will do so on their own at some point in an application. Some job notices list these areas of expertise, especially for collection managers and registrars who must know various cataloguing systems.

For maintenance employees, a familiarity or expertise with certain equipment, machinery, and vehicles is mandatory. Table saws, snow plows, and lawn mowers come to mind. In the arena of exhibit design and installation, graphic design programs are essential as are certain tool skills for making and installing exhibitions.

When answering this question, be aware that those you talk to may not be very technologically savvy or experienced. Older generations are often accused of this ignorance, but it extends across the age spectrum. Similarly, be careful not to encourage the idea that a museum's notoriety will be magically enhanced through the wonders of modern technology. Technology is a tool. Like any other tool, its effectiveness depends on how it is used, by whom, when, where, and why.

Question: What has been your experience with volunteers, trustees, and contractors?

Because of the collaborative nature of museums, few jobs are exempt from interpersonal encounters on a daily basis. Working with colleagues on the job is a given, but often staff are associated with volunteers, trustees, contractors, and the like. If you are not asked this question in an interview, you may want to bring it up yourself.

Non-museum staff who interact with staff can be terrific assets, or problematic. The last thing employers want are employees who have difficulty working with non-museum employees. Any evidence you can provide that supports your successful experience in this regard will be appreciated and helpful to your application. It can be listed on a résumé but, again, as an interview discussion point, it will have more impact.

Question: Why do you want to leave your current job (if you have one)?

This is one of the most important questions any job candidate is asked during an employment application process. There are several potential responses. For you personally, they would include: "I want the new job because it is an opportunity to advance within my field"; "It offers new professional possibilities"; "I can build upon what I have done in my career and advance it in a positive manner." For interviewers, you will want to emphasize how the new position seems ideally suited to your interests and abilities at this time in your career and life. You believe your experience will prove beneficial to the museum in general.

In explaining why you want to leave a job, make it a point to praise the institution you would leave behind. Note how well you have been treated there. Explain the good work you have done and the encouragement you receive.

Prospective employers appreciate and understand a candidate's job application when it has logical, positive roots.

If it is known that the museum you are leaving is in difficulty and that is mentioned by an interviewer, you can acknowledge this and politely note that those circumstances are contributing to various staff changes.

Personal, practical reasons for wanting a new job usually center around domestic changes such as a family move, divorce, closing of the job you are in, or the diminishment of the job's scope, funding, responsibilities, etc. These reasons may or may not raise red flags during an application process, although usually they are perfectly understandable.

Reasons that will immediately scuttle a job application are expressing a hatred for your current job or boss or colleagues, a dislike of the organization you are with, or a soured romantic affair at work. As previously noted, few museums will consider a candidate who is only trying to get away from a bad employment situation rather than being attracted to an excellent one. There are exceptions. Sometimes a museum is known as a terrible place to work, and other museums are perfectly happy to take staff away to its advantage. However, this is a rare circumstance.

Question: Have you visited our museum?

One piece of advice to offer museum job candidates is to visit the prospective museum before applying. This may seem obvious, but I was on a museum director search committee once where this did not happen for a couple of the candidates. They did a Skype interview and were only a state away from the museum in question, which could be easily reached in a few hours by train, car, or bus.

When visiting a prospective museum employer, think of the job you seek and how it fits the organization and how you would fit in. You can visit incognito or you may want to chat with people you encounter and say you are applying for such-and-such a position. What you observe and think about when visiting the museum will inform your interview nicely.

There will be occasions when visiting a prospective museum is impossible. These are usually caused by distance or schedule challenges. When logical, the prospective museum will understand. However, as with the example cited above, some situations are unacceptable and can reduce the chances of being hired.

If you have visited the museum with which you are interviewing, you can expect a variety of follow-up questions. What did you think of it? How were you treated by staff? What were some of its strengths and weaknesses? How long were you here? Etc. You can easily imagine what those interviewing you will ask.

Be careful about how you respond to questions regarding your visiting experience. If you are unreasonably critical, that may be met with suspicion regarding why you want to work there even if you really know what you are talking about. The last thing you want to convey in an interview is any sense that you are a troublemaker. Being too laudatory might also cause suspicion regarding the authenticity of your job application.

Obviously if you are an inside job candidate, your thoughts about the museum may be different from those being expressed by applicants who do not already work there. Be careful about how you express your opinions, ideas, and feelings about the museum. If you are too critical of those doing the interviewing, they may wonder why you are on staff already. If you are too blasé, interviewers may think you have little to offer.

Question: What would you say might be employment frustrations?

In the museum field, one popular answer to this question might be about pay, as it is often low. Skip that when being interviewed. You could comment on budget challenges as these limit funding for projects, work, and staffing. Limited resources and unreasonable expectations can be mentioned but only gently and in the context of how you overcome these challenges. Trustees can be fabulous or troublesome. You may want to avoid touching on this area.

Question: What would you say might be employment satisfactions?

It's hard to avoid speaking in clichés when answering this question. Presumably museum employees find their workplaces fascinating, enjoyable, meaningful, educational, uplifting, engaging, and rewarding environments. The idea that they exist for some public benefit is a core value for an employee.

There can be many satisfactory aspects of museum work including staff collegiality, individual learning, community service, legacy continuity, and pleasant surroundings. How one enumerates these will depend on individual candidate preferences as well as a sense of the interview's dynamics. Watching and listening to people at the meeting is essential in gauging how you and your words are being received.

Question: Define a museum.

This should be an easy question to answer, and one might wonder why it is asked. Individual responses will help interviewers get a better understanding of a candidate's perspectives on the field, why he or she is in it, and what priorities an employee will bring to a job. To a degree there is no right or wrong answer, just an informed opinion that summarizes one's reason for being in the museum field.

Question: Define this museum.

This question builds on the previous one but with the important specificity of being about the museum where you seek work. Depending on how it is asked and by whom, there may or may not be a right answer. A candidate will not know until asked, so watch and listen carefully when the inquiry is presented. Sometimes questions are asked in ways that imply or suggest particular answers.

Question: Where do you see yourself in five years?

This is an odd question that comes up on lists of questions to ask at job interviews. If I were asked, I'd likely say, "Alive." Fortunately, that has never happened. A job interview is no place to be a smartass. Yet, the inquiry has merit.

Because museums are very future focused and prospective employers have every reason to be curious about a job applicant's career plans, responding to the question can be expected and informative. Actually, it will probably be contained in some of the conversations that unfold during an interview anyway. As you explain your interest you will be discussing the future, though perhaps without referencing a formal annual schedule.

As an employer, I like to get a sense of how a job applicant would want to proceed once on the job. The goals and objectives might be less ambitious for a night guard position than that of a curator, but frankly, it is harder to find the former than the latter sometimes.

If this question or some variant of it is not asked, there is no need to introduce it with any major specificity.

Question: How do you handle personnel conflicts?

While the vast majority of museum employees are rarely embroiled in personal or professional conflicts, they do arise on occasion. There can be minor or major clashes in any workplace. While it is the job of management to deal with rifts, they sometimes cause them!

If you have good examples of how you have dealt with a personnel conflict, think about how you can explain them in a positive way that reflects well on your work ethic and camaraderie. If you have been fortunate enough to avoid such disruptions, you can explain that fact and why, in your opinion, it has been the case. People starting museum careers fall into this option.

Question: How do you like to learn on the job, and what sort of learning do you anticipate pursuing with the job you are applying for?

There are many ways of learning. They depend on the person learning and the nature of educational situations. You know how you learn best. Museums are hotbeds of teaching, both of the self and others. While education jobs are obviously central to this pursuit, few positions in museums are exempt from on-the-job pedagogical opportunities.

This is another one of those questions that is asked and answered in various ways during a job interview. Certainly, questions about why you are in the museum field, what you like about it, and how the work satisfies you will no doubt touch on or be all about learning. The educational quotient celebrated in all museums is obvious for the public served. It may not be so obvious for staff, yet they are often the most consistent and happy beneficiaries of the object-and-subject-based learning museums excel at.

Question: Tell us about any fundraising experience you have had.

While some museum jobs would appear to be far removed from having to raise any money for the institution, the idea is being promoted for all staff. Janitors might be a good example of people usually not required to raise money. However, these folks will be called upon to explain annual budget needs and asked if they have any ideas of sources of money. Curators, collection managers, media personnel, and visitor services people might have excellent connections to potential funding sources. Obviously, if you are asked this question and you have no experience, say so, but also be prepared to be asked if you would have any problem making suggestions once on the job.

Question: What sort of budgeting experience have you had?

A museum's annual budgeting process increasingly involves more employees than was once the case. This is especially true for smaller institutions. Participation in the budgeting process may be ancillary and involve only expressing cost needs. If you have not been part of such a process, say so, but be ready to welcome suggestions of participation. Be prepared to explain how the position you are applying for would be involved.

"CATCHALL" QUESTIONS

Everyone is usually well behaved during a job interview. Occasionally, there will be persons present who play the devil's advocate or take it upon themselves to "ask the tough questions." Museums can attract unwanted publicity or controversies over issues such as deaccessioning, diversity, funding, and personnel management. Depending on the job, applicants may be asked legitimate questions about their experience or perspectives in these arenas. How the questions are framed and presented will tell you much about a museum. You need to be prepared for surprises. Remain unflustered while projecting a highly professional and knowledgeable demeanor. If the subject is outside your expertise or experience, say so.

QUESTIONABLE QUESTIONS

Many questions are illegal (check local, state, and federal employment laws), inappropriate, too personal, or of questionable hiring relevance. How, or if, you answer these or variants of them will depend on: your feelings at the time; how such questions are asked; and what you know about local laws and customs. Regardless of notifications that a museum is an "equal opportunity employer," these and other interview questions might still be offered in ignorance or by accident. This can often be the case when interviewing with a museum that has a certain obvious racial, ethnic, religious, gender, or other identity mission. Below is only a partial list of such questions.

- Are you married? If so, to what sort of spouse—male, female, transgender . . . ?
- Are you divorced?
- If you are not married, do you have a "partner," and could you describe what that means? How does he or she fit into your career plans?
- Do you have kids? Your own, foster, adopted?
- If so, how many, and what are their ages?
- If not, are you planning to?
- Who takes care of your kids, and will that require time off?
- Does your spouse or "significant other" work?
- What does your spouse, partner, significant other do?
- What is your race?
- What is your ethnicity?
- What is your gender?
- Where will you live if you get this job?

- There is a large age difference between you and most of the staff here. Would that be a problem?
- What's your sign?
- How long do you anticipate working before you seek a new job or retire?
- What are your politics?
- Do you have any physical or mental handicaps?
- What is your religion, if you have one?
- Do you drink?
- What sort of recreational drugs do you use?
- Are you comfortable reporting to a male/female boss?
- Will you agree to a background check, including a lie detector test?
- Are you an American citizen?
- Where were you born?
- How is your health?

While some of the above questions may not be illegal, they are often avoided by employers to guard against potential charges of discrimination during or following a job application process. The nature of employment rules and mores changes as societal perspectives change. If a job search is being handled by a search firm, presumably the firm is well aware of contemporary requirements regarding acceptable and unacceptable interview procedures, including questions to be asked by the employer and the applicant.

CONCLUSION

Most museum employment interview questions are logical and appropriate. This is an excellent first opportunity to be personally frank while showing enthusiasm and respect for the institution and those you are meeting with. In most situations, you will have never met the person or persons who interview you. These conversations are the "get acquainted" time for a relationship that may or may not grow. Regardless, you and the people with whom you meet will now be new friends, and even if you are not hired, that acquaintanceship may continue well beyond the particular job application process. This is one reason to guard against giving "canned" answers to interview questions. These can throw conversations off and truly alienate prospective employers. Be honest, candid, informative, and friendly throughout your interview process! As noted elsewhere in this book, the museum field remains small enough for individual reputations to be readily researched. You want yours to always be stellar!

Chapter Seven

You Interview the Museum

A job interview should be a two-way conversation: a museum interviews a candidate and a candidate interviews a museum. This chapter deals with the latter.

QUESTIONS TO ASK AT THE FIRST INTERVIEW

There are many questions candidates should ask about a possible job. They will depend on the nature of the museum, the position, and the interview. Answers to many of the questions can be sought outside the confines of a typical interview. Many of your potential questions will probably be covered during your research about the museum and at the interview(s). Although interviewers generally will ask you if you have any questions, you will probably not have time to ask all of your questions during your (first) interview. Asking good (and relevant) questions will show genuine interest in the job.

Many of the questions listed here will already have been answered either in the interview or from your research, so obviously you won't want to ask them if you already know the answers. Additionally, you should consider additional inquiries other than those listed here.

Question: What is the museum looking for in seeking to fill this position?

Listen closely to the responses and study body language. Different people in the conversation may have different ideas. Do these correspond to what you think the job is or should be? You may want to interject your thoughts on the job description.

Question: Who does the position report to?

A person's boss or bosses are perhaps the most important individuals affecting one's employment satisfaction, success, failure, mental stability, happiness, and future. We will not always agree with our supervisors all the time, but conversely, if they have bad reputations as managers, be cautious about proceeding with a job application. Do not think you can change them. On the other hand, good or excellent bosses are worth their weight in gold.

Question: What employees, volunteers, contract workers, etc. might, or will, I be responsible for?

A job may or may not entail managing others in a structured manner, but in the museum field all sorts of individuals can be involved who require supervision. Even if the job you seek is not a supervisory one on a constant basis, there may be occasions when you are a boss. If, on the other hand, the job does involve handling one or more employees, be sure of your authority, duties, and support to handle them as professionally appropriate.

Question: What sort of audiences does the museum serve, and is there any interest in changing or expanding them? If so, how might that happen? Is success determined by attendance figures?

Museums are concerned about defining audiences both to serve them better and to increase them. A plural designation is good to use as few (no?) museums have only one audience. It should be interesting to hear the response to this question though it may be a topic of discussion already included in the interview process, not to mention noted in the job description itself.

Measuring success, unfortunately, remains a statistical game of participation numbers. Be careful to listen for words like metrics, rubrics, models, bottom line, outcomes, measures, etc. You may have to apply this sort of numerical coding to your reports and record keeping. Success in museums is also measured by how much publicity a program, activity, exhibition, etc. gets.

Question: How would you characterize the work atmosphere at the museum?

This is a question asked carefully, and you may even want to avoid it. Of course, the response will be "excellent," and that may very well be true. There are more informal ways to inquire during casual conversations that are not part of a formal interview. Actually, you may learn more from idle chitchat than from precise discussions.

Question: How would you describe the resources available for this position?

This is a polite way of asking what you will have to work with to do your job. It encompasses more than funding for whatever you want, have, or need to do. Museums that are government-owned or are part of larger institutions, such as colleges and universities, may have more options for employees than private museums that have to live on their own budgets.

Question: What happened to the person who had the position previously?

I was the fourth director in ten years for Boscobel Restoration Inc., a historic house museum in Garrison, NY. This question had great relevance to me when I was asked to interview for the job. It was not answered directly or clearly by the trustees during my several interviews, but research had revealed the answer. And, I was able to talk to the three previous directors. I quickly learned why there was such turnover (my predecessor had been there nine months). In accepting the job, I was able to take corrective action with several staff and trustee changes. Things improved dramatically, though two important changes remained to be made when I retired.

In most cases, people who leave museum jobs do so on good terms and to advance their careers, relocate for personal reasons, or retire. It is always helpful to chat with these folks when applying for their jobs. This may not be necessary when applying from within the museum in which you already work. If there is a reluctance to discuss the departure of an employee, do not press the issue, but be mindful of potential problems should you be the successful replacement.

Question: If it is a new position, why is it being created? Is it in the annual budget?

New jobs can be exciting. They offer great potential to start something that was never done or not done well. Presumably you will have certain liberties to be creative and even experimental. Be careful to avoid agreeing to unrealistic expectations, however. And, get a sense about how seriously committed the museum is to sustaining the position over time.

Question: What roles do trustees play in museum operations, if any?

Depending on the size of a museum and how it accomplishes its work, trustees can be involved in operational matters to a degree that ranges from extremely helpful to destructive. This tends to happen less is large museums though there are exceptions, especially regarding fundraising. Those seeking employment in development offices need to be especially mindful as trustees will almost certainly assist, lead, interfere with, or otherwise participate in raising money for the museum.

Inquiring about trustee involvement in a museum's operations must be approached diplomatically so as not to offend or throw an interview off course. To say or imply concern over the practice will cause suspicion. To enthusiastically embrace the idea can sound like the candidate may be speaking in a disingenuous manner simply to get the job.

There are two ways to submit this question: openly at a formal interview, which, depending on the position may or may not include a trustee(s); or, quietly in person-to-person inquiries with staff.

Question: Are there annual performance reviews; if so, who does them, and are these linked to salary increases?

The old days of simply being hired and never subjected to formal job reviews in some official capacity are pretty much over for most museums. This is especially true for large institutions. The structure for reviews will vary. Usually one's boss leads them in accord with an organization's policies and procedures on implementation. This includes how and when to implement one. Depending on the job, only one person might be the reviewer. In the case of directors, more than one will participate.

Reviews are usually done annually. There is a form and format for the process. There should be a list of topics to discuss relating to how well an employee is doing his or her work as spelled out in the job description. The review should be a conversational exchange between the employee and the boss. Key points will be documented and contained in staff personnel files. The review will usually be signed by both the reviewer and the person being reviewed. Job applicants need not dwell on the minutiae of any review process, but asking about it will do two things: it will indicate the level of professionalism of the museum; and it will signal an applicant's understanding of current and expected employment procedures. The signed review is a confidential document to be retained in an employee's personnel file for no one but designated staff to see.

Question: How would you describe the financial health of the museum? May I see the annual budget? The most recent audit?

Museums are financially precarious organizations, yet they rarely close. This speaks volumes about their value and the devotion of those responsible for leading them. It is always a good idea when interviewing to ask about how an institution is doing fiscally. The question can easily be worded in ways that hardly suggest suspicious thoughts.

The amount of involvement museum employees have with financial matters depends on one's job. Obviously, fundraising staff are critical to agreeing upon, setting, and meeting money-raising goals. An entry-level maintenance person will be far out of the financial loop. When it comes to the financial health of a museum, most staff need to help assure cost controls.

A museum's budget is the annual operating plan approved in advance by a board of trustees to meets its mission. It will not include everything everyone wants, and, in fact, much will be left out. The lion's share of the budget will be for employee compensation. Studying a museum budget tells volumes about the organization.

Job applicants may ask to see a museum's current annual budget, but the question needs to be worded carefully. Something like, "Is it customary for job applicants to be given a copy of the museum's annual budget?" might be received without suspicion. If you are successful in getting the budget, study it closely. If peculiarities pop out or you are confused, you may or may not have the opportunity to ask questions later. If you are working through a search firm, discuss the subject with them.

Most museums have independent audits done every year. The goal is to have a "clean audit." This means the outside investigators found nothing irregular about the financial operations of the institution. Every museum I have worked in has gotten one, every year. Sometimes there can be anomalies. They either result from a temporary situation a museum is dealing with (as might happen in a sudden recession or with a debt load issue), or the audit firm did not understand an aspect of an institution's operations. If you are able to see an audit, pay close attention to the footnotes. Sometimes they contain some of the most interesting and telling stories about a museum.

You do not want to work at a museum that does not have an independent audit done, annually at best.

Question: How would you describe the staff and the work atmosphere?

This is something of an open-ended question. Mostly you will get a positive response. Be they trustee or staff, no one will say so-and-so is a jerk, nasty, lazy, incompetent, etc. In most museums, staff and board are collegial, respectful, and supportive to one degree or another. Maintenance workers who do the heavy lifting, literally, are always appreciated because few others will, can, or should be doing this work. On the other hand, there may be little understanding of what curators do.

You might want to ask if there have been any personnel disruptions or staff job actions recently. Again, the question can be worded politely in the following manner: "Given what we read about in the press regarding employee actions against employers and vice versa, have there been any instances here that candidates for this job should know about? If there have been, may candidates ask about them?

Question: Does the museum take any political positions, and if so, how are they pursued? What sort of staff participation in politics is allowed either in private or on the job?

Given the often rigid differences between Americans regarding their political views now, how these play out in the workplace can be important insofar as employment is concerned. Museums are, by nature, very conservative endeavors when it comes to expressing any opinions that may in the least be considered political.

Because so many topics today are explained, interpreted, or felt to reflect certain political views, museum employees have to exercise great care to avoid disruptive conflicts. Some issues, such as equal rights for anyone identifying as a member of the LGBT community, have been supported by museums largely because there are so many of these folks working in or being served by museums. Occasionally issues relating to the protection of art and historic artifacts against assault by totalitarian groups are supported. Again, museums have a special interest in these things. And, American museums will lobby for government support of funding for museums of all sorts.

Museums usually do not support political parties, candidates, or campaigns. Staff may, but proselytizing on the job, or with museum facilities and equipment, is frowned upon.

Question: What is the hiring plan for this position; in other words, when does the museum hope to fill it, and how will candidates be kept informed about the process?

These questions are pretty self-evident, but if you have not been told, it does no harm to ask. It might be best to inquire at the end of the interview. Remember to be sure that the employer has easy access to you during the entire application process, whether to you personally or through a search firm. If any of your contact information changes during this process, alert all who need to know right away.

Sometimes hiring takes longer than a museum might anticipate. If you are anxious about a lack of communication during an application process, you can contact the museum for information. This can be done easily and without worry: an email or phone call saying you remain excited about the job and want to check in on the hiring process. Your contact information remains the same. If more information is needed, you are happy to provide it. Thank you very much.

When working through a search firm, the firm should know the answer to this question and keep you informed during the entire application process.

Question: What is the salary and benefit package?

This is a question best asked toward the end of the first interview. The information may be included in a job announcement, especially if the museum is government-owned and operated (federal, state, or local). Because museum work is considered cause-related and mission-focused, money is not always discussed as a key factor when applying for work. This notion may be silly, but few museums want employees who are there simply to have a job. However, the information is obviously essential. Employers are hardly put off by the inquiry, but they may be if it is the first one an applicant asks.

To be sure, lousy compensation can be a deal breaker, especially in museums. These organizations tend to pay on the low end for most positions. And, they often provide minimal benefits. Young, entry-level staff might not have the financial needs of older individuals with domestic costs to cover. This can work to candidates' advantages or disadvantages. It is one reason for job turnover. Learning if a person left a job because of weak compensation can be informative for applicants.

Benefit packages will vary from museum to museum. It is important to know what is included, especially for health coverage. If an applicant has a family, how can they be included if desired? Health plans can be complicated and costly to staff as well as the museum. You might not have time at a first interview to learn about the details of coverage, but there may be documentation a museum can share with candidates.

In addition to health coverage, there will often be a retirement plan, vacation, personal days, and holiday schedule, and even support for professional education. These are usually explained in personnel policies.

Find out how flexible compensation may be. For example, vacation and personal days can sometimes be added to in exchange for accepting what might be low pay.

You may or may not want to ask about whether freelance work is permitted for personal income. Some museums allow it, but most frown on it. Writing may fall into this category, as curators in particular are often book authors.

Question: What is the work schedule for this position?

Most museum jobs follow a customary forty-hour work week. However, that week may vary to include one or two weekend days. Evenings are also times for some work, at some jobs. Maintenance, education, security, public relations, visitor services, and earned income jobs that involve face-to-face encounters with the public often happen outside Monday through Friday 9:00 a.m. to 5:00 p.m. schedules. Notices for museum employment of this kind will often state the varying schedules.

Museum employees who have regular weekday work hours need to know how or if they are compensated for working outside those hours. Is that compensation financial or done with time? This should be spelled out in personnel manuals, but it does no harm to ask.

Learn about requirements that your position fills in for absent employees. This would be the case with sales shop associates, admission desk staff, and maintenance and security employees. Are these required assignments or optional, and how are they compensated for?

But, because museums are usually open to the public on weekends and some evenings, and they have many special events, certain positions require scheduling flexibility. This is especially true for visitor services personnel as well as maintenance and security employees. Educators, curators, and public relations staff are usually on duty for events that involve their respective departments or the museum as a whole. Depending on the size of the museum, directors are almost always on call. The smaller the museum, the more activities, events, programs, etc., they attend. The larger the museum, the less they may need to be present.

Question: Is it expected or permissible to work virtually, and if so, can the employer describe this sort of arrangement?

Depending on a particular museum job, working off-site can be an option. Instructions about this will usually be contained in personnel manuals. Positions that require writing and research, which is certainly the case with curating, may request time outside the museum for such activity. How is this requested? Who monitors it? How is it reported?

Question: What facilities, equipment, and material support are there for the position?

During a job application process, and especially when being interviewed, try to get a sense of what equipment and material support you will have to do your job. In addition to physical evidences of these necessities, what, if any, other staff assistance will you have? A good example now involves information technology. What is the hardware and software like? Who is on call for technical assistance? How much are you expected to know?

Beyond IT needs, maintenance staff must know what equipment they have available, be it vehicles, machinery, tools, etc. Who is responsible for the equipment, what safety measures are in place? What employee expertise is expected for the equipment?

Question: Is travel involved, locally or long-distance?

Some museum jobs require travel more than others. Security positions rarely call for staff to venture far from a museum. Curators, fundraisers, and certainly directors will travel. Museum employment ads may or may not reference travel requirements. If they do not, you should ask anyway. If they do, then questions about this aspect of the job are perfectly acceptable and accepted.

Travel can range from going around the corner to around the globe. It is important to know who requires it, why, and who monitors it. How is it paid for, and how are you as an employee paid for the time? What if you are unable to meet a travel request? If it is by car, are you expected to use your own, and if so, how are you compensated for that?

Question: Are there regularly scheduled staff or other meetings to attend, and what would this position's role be?

Organizing one's work schedule is essential for effective employment. How time is allotted to do what, and when, is a matter of personal and professional choice as well as outside forces. Because museums are group efforts, meetings occur. How often depends on the institution, one's job, and what projects are planned, underway, or concluding. A security night guard may need to attend few meetings, while a director will be at many.

Though not at the top of any list of interview questions, the subject of meetings can be revealing. Some people like them; some hate them. Participation may be required or optional. When participation is expected, what does that mean? For instance, museums often have regularly scheduled staff meetings. These can require reports from offices, individuals, departments, etc. Sometimes these reports will be written or simply spoken. Regardless, the more a job applicant knows, the better.

Question: Is there a dress code?

In 1970 there was a dress code at Tiffany & Co. in New York City forbidding women from wearing slacks on the job. Recognizing that fashions were changing, after much discussion, the company decided it was permissible if the slacks were part of a suit ensemble and were purchased at the conservative and upscale department store B. Altman, with which Tiffany's had a discount arrangement for men's clothing. Prospective museum employees should inquire about any employee dress requirements. Again, this should not be a top-priority question, and indeed, it will no doubt be contained in a personnel manual.

Clothing worn on a museum job will tend to reflect the job. Male maintenance staff will rarely be seen in suits and ties. But, they may have uniforms to wear, as might security personnel. If applying for these jobs, ask about uniforms and how they are paid for, cared for, and replaced. Some museums tend to be more formal when it comes to how men and women in positions of authority dress. Whether or not men wear ties will depend on personal preference, a particular job, and institutional requirements. For men or women, cleavage is usually a no-no.

Personal hygiene is equally important. How to ask about this will be a delicate matter. While it may be noted in a personnel manual, affronts are usually dealt with on a case by case basis. For men, beards were once banned. That changed years ago. Indeed, the author has had a beard since 1971. Body odor remains disliked. Certainly, be mindful of these matters when interviewing. No one wants to lose a job because of a wardrobe malfunction or offensive personal aroma.

Question: How does this position fit into the budget and annual budget planning?

All museum jobs are part of an institution's budget. They are calculated annually. If the museum is relatively secure financially, most jobs will be relatively secure. There will on occasion be temporary experimental positions or ones established for projects such as exhibitions. Presumably any employment discussions will explain clearly the nature of the job vis-à-vis an organization's overall work plan. It must be clear where the job is placed within the larger scheme of operations.

Should there be any doubt, it is perfectly acceptable for a job applicant to ask if the position is a permanent one. The question might be worded along the following lines: "May I reconfirm that this is a permanent position, subject, of course, to the usual personnel regulations?" Be careful of the word *permanent* though. If that is put in writing an employee may think he or she has a job for life. Wrong. While the museum may hope the post is permanent, change can happen.

In determining how a job fits within a museum, it is important to listen for financial obligations that may influence its longevity. For example, a sales shop manager may be expected (if not required) to meet certain sales objectives. Because the magnitude of shop sales will depend, to some degree, on the number of visitors a museum receives, financial goals can be difficult to achieve if visitation is not robust.

It is also good to know if the job is involved in budget planning. This means setting numbers for annual budgeting processes. Does the position involve participation in this, or not? There are no preferences in this regard, but it is very important to know. If budgeting is part of the duties, you will be asked about your experience in this regard.

If you have looked up the museum on GuideStar, Charity Navigator, or a similar nonprofit rating source and have any comments as a result, you may want to express them. Some museums will not be listed on these, such as government-owned and -operated institutions.

Question: Is there a personnel manual, and if so, may I have a copy?

As with most businesses of any size, museums now customarily have personnel manuals, handbooks, employee policy statements, or a formal document of this nature, approved by the board of trustees, usually with legal input. They are extremely important for employees and employers. Good manuals outline, often in some detail, the directives, benefits, expectations, and procedures staff need to abide by and follow on (and sometimes off) the job.

Personnel manuals will include work hours, benefits, a holiday schedule, dress code (if any), applicable reporting structures, whistle blower policy, grievance procedures, pay schedules, annual performance review procedures, and matters relating to overtime, contract work, expenditure, off-site work allowances, etc. Presumably personnel manuals are updated annually or when pertinent employment changes take effect, as might happen with retirement plans and other benefits. The personnel manual is usually not a contract and should not be considered such. Some museums are clear about this, while others see no need to mention it.

Because museum trustees are not employees, most museum personnel manuals do not include instructions for these volunteers. Expected behavior might occasionally be found in "trustee job descriptions" and "conflict of interest forms," though these are not as common as one would hope. It may do no harm to ask in an interview if they exist, but that might be a question best left for the end of the conversation if there is time, or it may be folded into discussions about the board in general.

If a candidate for a museum job can obtain a copy of the current personnel manual, that will be of great value. When working through a search firm or for a government museum job, this may be easy. When applying on one's own, simply request it as part of your process. Be cautious about your job interest if the museum a) does not have a manual; b) refuses to share it with you as a candidate; or c) the manual is not done very well.

If you get a copy of the current personnel manual, examine it carefully. Remember, these are the employment rules you have to accept and abide by. They are no substitute for your job description. They amplify it.

Question: Are there other governance documents I should have?

As previously noted, when researching a museum, it will be helpful to have documents regarding who governs it; what formal and officially directed policies are in place; and certain procedural matters one needs to be aware of. These will differ between private and government-owned museums. For example, a county-owned museum may not have articles of incorporation, but it should have legal documentation authorizing its formation or acceptance into the government authority.

Documents of value when doing research on a museum job at a private (non-government) institution will include the following (some may be impossible to get, such as board meeting minutes or the annual budget):

- A 990, which is basically an annual tax return
- Current bylaws
- Articles of incorporation, if relevant and in existence
- The minutes of a recent board of trustees meeting
- An annual report, if one is done
- The latest annual budget, approved by the board of trustees
- A current staff organization chart
- Any relevant codes or operating policies
- The most recent annual audit
- The most recent board approved strategic or long-range plan

When applying for a job on your own, some of the above may be difficult if not impossible to get. If you are working through a search firm, it may be easier.

INTERVIEWING THE MUSEUM COMMUNITY

Museums usually realize their public service mission through community programming of some sort. That programming can be exhibitions; education activities; research and scholarly access to collections and staff; and preserving objects of importance to various audiences or groups, be they of a community or not. Depending on the museum you want to work in, part of your interview research should involve its community, however that is defined.

Typically, community is defined geographically, yet many museums may not focus on the neighborhood they are in. The Metropolitan Museum of Art is hardly devoting the lion's share of its programming to those living around its location at Fifth Avenue and 81st Street. Museums, especially those in small towns and the suburbs, are often engaged in serving their geographical communities, usually with education and other social programming. Museums in rural out-of-the-way places may have no local audiences to serve.

As you define a museum's community, ask others what they think of it. You might want to know if people are aware of the museum, visit it, use its services, take guests to it, join it as members, or support its education work. Answers to these questions can inform a job candidate and enliven the face-to-face interview conversation.

"Interviewing" a community about a museum located in its midst is not difficult if you have the time and can talk to people face to face. Inquiries might be made of people who work in restaurants, a library, grocery store, cab drivers, gas station, schools, or other public venues. This might be easy in a small town where the museum is in its midst. The options will be fewer for a museum in a rural area where few people live or work nearby. The opposite will be the case in a big city. Nevertheless, a few well-chosen conversations can provide helpful information. If none is forthcoming, that need not reflect poorly on the museum in question. Most people are not regular museum visitors. Some never visit.

SECOND INTERVIEWS

If you are called back for a second interview—congratulations! Obviously, something went right at your first interview. But, *do not think you have the job.* Usually at least two people are being called back. Review everything you planned for and did in the first interview. Presumably you have sent notes of appreciation to key individuals you met with for the first interview. Such communications can be mailed in hard copy or submitted online, as you deem appropriate. If appropriate, answer any questions that came up during that time. Perhaps supply the interview team with materials that might amplify the conversation you had.

Whether it is the first or second (or third!) interview, follow-up is important. It must be done quickly. Letting days elapse before responding is unwise and suggests you are not committed to the job or have other matters of more pressing interest to attend to. Comments can be simple expressions of your appreciation for the courtesy of a meeting. They can, and usually are, more substantive as you touch on various points discussed. During an interview it is helpful to take notes, and hardly a suspect activity. (Of course, do not record the meeting.) Your response must avoid being a thesis. Succinctly include subjects you think were of obvious importance. If you are responding to a first interview and another might be possible, express how much you would look forward to that. Let your references know about your interview. Any information you can provide them should be helpful if they are contacted. Should that happen, they can be directed to say how much you enjoyed your interview and that you are even more excited about the job.

For a second interview you are in a much better position than you were when you first met with the museum search team. Regardless, review all the advice contained in this book. The last thing you want is to make a mistake, deviate unpredictably, or quizzically contradict the efforts you are devoting to this job application.

Because you have already met with people at the hiring museum, you will be more comfortable in this second discussion. Be prepared for the interview team to possibly expand in number. It is not unusual for museums to have group meetings rather than one-on-one encounters. There may or may not be a trustee or two present. You may be asked the same questions that were asked in the first interview, and you may have the same questions you had in the first interview but perhaps rephrased. If you can get the names of the second interview team and any who are new to you, learn about them before you meet.

Having talked with you already, presumably the museum has done more research about your work. Staff or trustees from the museum may have even been able to visit where you are currently employed. Hopefully they will not have mentioned why they were there! In the second interview, there will be references to what you said at the first one. This is why contemporaneous notes you made during and immediately after that can be helpful. Review these.

Based on what transpired in the first get-together, and on thoughts you have afterwards, if you have additional questions about the museum, perhaps colleagues can help answer them. *The museum profession is full of people who know people and you never know who knows whom.* Any and all sleuthing that a job candidate does before, during, and after a job interview is time well spent.

WHAT TO DO IF HIRED

When you are a successful job candidate, there are certain professional and procedural protocols that usually kick in. But first congratulate yourself! Your credentials, persona, and hard work as an applicant were clearly appreciated and effective. For most positions you will be personally notified of your success by someone in authority at the museum. This can happen face to face or by phone. Email, text, and other social media are too informal and impersonal for most institutions. Hold off on any public announcement until you get the offer in writing and you have responded in writing. If the hire is newsworthy, the museum will explain how it handles such media alerts. The notification is the start of a new professional relationship in your life. Get off on the right foot and follow the institution's lead.

If you are resigning from a current museum job, you owe your present employer the courtesy of an immediate explanation about your pending departure. How you handle this is important to support your professional reputation. I am happy to say that I can return to any of the six museums where I have worked and be welcomed. Your transition will set the pace for such a future. You will presumably be asked to help the institution with any information or housekeeping matters relating to your work there. Both those you will leave behind and those coming after you will appreciate all your input. Obviously if this is your first museum job you need not consider this "resignation advice." But, do not forget it later in your career as you change jobs.

When you are told you are the successful job candidate, you should expect to discuss when you can start. Most employers understand this will vary depending on an individual's and the institution's schedules. When I was hired to join the curatorial staff at the Museum of The City of New York, I was sent a short letter confirming this good news. It listed my salary ($6,000) and a commencement date that was six months away. The date aligned with the museum's fiscal year and the start of my job (which was new) in the budget cycle. I had no problem with this as I could live at home and prepare for my move to the city. By the time I was told of my hire, I had agreed to the employment terms. However, there may be room for negotiation if you are the successful candidate. This conversation would obviously relate to salary and benefits but also how the job is defined within the larger organization. Usually such discussions do not end in either the candidate or the museum rejecting the other, but it has to be considered as a possibility. Either before you start a new job or immediately upon arrival, with social security card in hand, you will (or should) be required to fill out various employment documents. Most of these relate to salary confirmation and banking deposits, medical, insurance and retirement benefits. You may have to agree to and sign a personnel manual.

Finally, if, during the application process, or at its conclusion, you have decided the job is not for you or you have taken another one, please tell the prospective employer right away. It is unfair to the institution or your reputation to keep everyone hanging while you dillydally considering other options.

WHAT TO DO IF YOU DON'T GET THE JOB

Despite all of your efforts, you find out that you don't get the job. The museum should notify you of their decision. While disappointed (or not, if you were not keen on the job), you should follow up politely to thank the museum/those who interviewed you, for considering you for the job, and also to obtain information about why you did not get the job. This will help you with future job applications. This includes

- By phone, email, or mail, thank the person(s) you interviewed with. You can do this even when you worked through a search firm, but ask their advice first.
- If you can, find out why you were not hired, do so, as it can help as you move forward.
- Never argue with a potential employer if you are not hired.
- Sometimes positions reopen not long after they are filled, as mistakes can be made. It is permissible to reapply if you wish, but never reference the failed hiring that may have caused the repeated vacancy. If the reason is discussed by the employer, you can respond as you wish but caution is advised.
- You can do a lot of the above even if you were an applicant being considered from within a particular museum.

CONCLUSION

Deciding how or if you wish to "interview a museum" will vary depending on the museum in question, the job you are seeking, and your comfort level initiating inquiries during the application process. Employers appreciate and respect good questions presented in interviews. In fact, the better the question(s), the more impressive the applicant. Museums should devote considerable attention to learning as much as is legally permitted about a candidate. If this is not the case, unless a person is well known to a museum, hiring mistakes occur. Conversely, employment seekers must do all they can to investigate the museum where they hope to work. Inquiries are always of value, so do not be a shy applicant.

Chapter Eight

Museum Job Search Variables

The employment processes outlined in the previous chapters are customary. Most museums implement them as described, and most applicants follow them as directed. There are a few alternate routes to seeking museum jobs. These include working exclusively and only with search firms; changing careers to enter the field; and being aware of current demographics as they influence the workplace.

WORKING WITH A SEARCH FIRM

Museums often use private employment firms when seeking to fill positions. These are usually for executive jobs rather than rank and file posts such as maintenance or security staff. As noted previously, currently those with expertise in the museum job world include

- Arts Consulting Group, http://artsconsulting.com/
- Management Consultants for the Arts, https://www.mcaonline.us/
- Museum Management Consultants, Inc., http://museum-management.com/
- m/Oppenheim, https://www.moppenheim.com/
- Opportunity Resources, Inc., https://www.opportunityresources.net/
- Russell Reynolds Associates, http://www.russellreynolds.com/

Visiting their websites will explain what they do and how. They usually list current clients as well as recent positions they have filled. You can approach these firms directly to discuss your personal job searches, or you will need to contact them if so instructed in a museum's classified listings. Generally speaking, trying to work around a contracted search firm is inadvisable.

The firms cited above have considerable experience in the nonprofit sector, which is why they are involved with museum hiring projects. I have worked with a few of these, both when being sought for a job and in seeking a job. My experience has been positive. They know what they are doing even if at times you may wonder. Once in their hands, you need to pretty much follow their instructions.

A search firm's job is to cause a successful search. To this end, they spend a lot of time with the museum leadership that hires them, and they study candidates closely. The last thing a firm wants is a failed search. Problems that may erupt along the way usually result from disagreements with a firm and the museum that hired them. As a candidate, your best course of action is to remain on the sidelines should disputes happen. Again, these are rare, but one needs to be on guard.

Maintaining a good rapport with a search firm will do you no harm. You may or may not be a successful candidate for a job, but a firm will have gotten to know you well. They tend to remain alert to potential applicants for jobs they are hired to fill. Over time, you may even want to periodically update a firm with whom you have worked, on the progress of your career.

A LATERAL CAREER MOVE

A lateral career move usually involves changing professional fields altogether. For example, a corporate CEO who has been in the business sector only may decide she or he would prefer to run a museum. A dealer in antiques or art may want to be a curator. Or, a public school teacher might prefer to be a museum educator. Obviously, there may or may not be parallels between occupations.

It is also not uncommon for the museum field to attract people with no experience whatsoever in the various disciplines outlined in this book. There have been instances when a corporate CEO thinks she can be a curator, or a bus driver will aspire to run a gift shop. Where once these silly job shifts might have been possible, today, given the increased professionalism of the museum world, these sorts of options are few. This is a positive development.

In common with many professions, the established museum order is skeptical about outsiders wanting to transition into the fold. It is easy if your expertise is in building maintenance, accounting, or security, but for jobs that require knowing about certain liberal arts academic subjects and objects, and other areas of museum work, people within them can be skeptical.

In 2008, when the Great Recession hit, a friend of mine who had her own search firm specializing in cultural institutions would receive phone calls from men who had lost their jobs in the finance industry. They thought their abilities and experience would translate well for museum jobs such as directing or curating. She responded that because she had a bank account would that qualify her to be a bank president? The conversations were very short.

Nevertheless, if you are seriously contemplating moving into the museum field from another line of work, consider the following questions:

- Why do you want to do this?
  - Do museums excite you?
  - If so, how and why do they attract you?
  - What aspect of them appeals to your intellect and emotional well-being?
  - Do you visit them often, and if so, what sorts of museums do you like?
  - Can you shift your current livelihood and/or domestic situation to pursue your passion without complications that will impede success in your new field?
- Have you talked to museum professionals regarding your plans?
  - What advice have they given you?
  - Will you continue such conversations as you proceed to shift careers?
- Are you or have you been a member of a museum(s)?
- Are you or have you been a member of a museum professional organization such as the American Alliance of Museums, the American Association for State and Local History, or a regional organization of this type?
- What transferable skills do you think you have that museums could really use?
  - In analyzing the typical museum jobs, as listed in this book or elsewhere, which ones appeal to you? Which ones do you think would be suitable to the work you have been doing?
- Will you be prepared to hear that your past or current employment may not be seen as helpful for a particular museum job?
- Most museum jobs are categorized within specialized career tracks in the larger field. As such, they usually require specifically relevant training, procedures, skills, and work applications. Will you be willing to "retrain" for a particular area of museum work?
- Will your current life circumstances be an issue for your desired career change?
  - Age?
  - Gender?
  - Ethnicity, race?
  - Citizenship status?

- ◦ Location?
- ◦ Partnership status?
- ◦ Family situation?
- ◦ Finances?
- ◦ Health, mental or physical?
- ◦ Education?
- How might museum compensation (salaries and benefits) compare to what is customary in the field you are now in?
  - ◦ Will that be a factor in your decision?
  - ◦ Do you have additional options for income, health insurance, and retirement programs that make up for what a museum might offer? For example, a retired police officer or firefighter will usually have a comfortable retirement and health package. This can allow a candidate to forego more pressing compensation needs when seeking a museum job.
- Can you structure your résumé to reflect your experience in ways that make sense for whatever museum job you are seeking now, without being disingenuous, cute, or incomprehensible?
- Are you willing to start at the bottom of whatever area you are interested in and work your way up?
- Are you willing to seek new academic degrees or certificates or other credentials expected of certain museum job applicants?
  - ◦ What will this require insofar as costs and time are concerned?
- Are you willing to report to supervisors who have different perspectives, motivations, and commitments than those to whom you might have reported in the past?
- Are you willing to understand the nature of the nonprofit sector and work with boards of trustees and on-the-job volunteers?
  - ◦ Museums are collaborative ventures in ways unlike companies. For example, they use volunteers in several important areas including on the job and for governance, by serving on a board of trustees.
- What sort of research have you done about museums in general or the specific one or type that you would like to work in? There are many books about museum work or aspects thereof. These can be found online and through such professional organizations as the American Alliance of Museums and the American Association for State and Local History.

PERSONAL DEMOGRAPHIC
IDENTITY AND MUSEUM JOBS

Museum job candidates must understand that not all employment parameters are explained in an institution's official documents, announcements, pronouncements, etc. This is apparent in generational differences on the job, but more importantly, during application processes. When seeking and considering jobs, it will not be unusual for a candidate to be younger than most of the people he or she will interview with. Studies have been done identifying various personality characteristics of various generations in America. The oldest of these are usually found on boards of trustees. They represent the Silent Generation, born between 1925 and 1945. The Baby Boomers, born between 1946 and 1964, are the employees most commonly encountered today in the museum field. It is a very large generation and still in its working years. However, Boomers are retiring and dying at a fast rate, so there will be much turnover in the next decade in particular. Most job applicants will represent Generation X (born between 1965 and 1979) and Y (born between 1980 and 2000). For the most part, Generation Z (born between 2000 and the present) is not yet in full-time job-hunting mode.

Diversity is a popular topic of conversation both inside and outside museums these days. The subject acknowledges inclusions and exclusions regarding race, gender, ethnicity, disability, religion, age, place of origin, education, political allegiance, you name it. Do museums include or exclude people based on these characteristics, or some aspects thereof? The people identified can be trustees, staff, donors, members, or the general public. Topics of discussion can be about museum exhibitions, programming, collections, and the mission of a particular museum. This reality has an impact on museum hiring practices.

There are laws about not hiring certain people for certain reasons. Laws about hiring people because of certain preferences are harder to find or define. Job seekers in the museum field need to take note of the demographic they represent, or identify with, and how that may or may not be accepted by the museum they are applying to. There are thousands of museums that are about a certain group of people or an aspect thereof, and thus their hiring practices could favor those groups. The group could be identified as Jewish, African American, Huguenot, female, Armenian, Native American, military, musicians, etc.

Occasionally a hiring brouhaha can erupt when outsiders think someone with the wrong personal demographic identity is hired. In 2018, the Brooklyn Museum hired a white scholar to be the consulting curator of African art. This was criticized by some black cultural and civic leaders. The museum stood by its decision and was supported by various black academics knowledgeable about the curator and the field of study.[1]

As a job applicant, do you need to be part of the group for which the museum exists? While there is probably nothing in any museum's governing and other written materials that specify required staff demographic identities for various jobs, the chances that a non-Native American will direct a museum about Native Americans is slim. Similarly, few Jewish museums will have directors who are not Jewish. Military museums may not have directors who did not serve in the military, and so on, at least insofar as leadership positions are concerned. Conforming to a museum's demographic identity may not matter when it comes to maintenance, exhibition design, or security staff.

The larger question about expansive demographic inclusion for job candidates is a key focus for museum employment practices today. With the exception of maintenance and security staff, the majority of museum employees are white. Most are female. This is changing; therefore, job candidates need to be aware of what "category" or "categories" they may represent and *if,* or *how,* that affects their application.[2]

DISCRIMINATION

The United States, and various states, has laws regarding employment discrimination. These are designed to protect people who may be unfairly treated because of gender, ethnicity, religion, race, age, etc. Most museum hiring takes place relatively fairly. But, applicants should be on guard nevertheless. Sometimes discrimination is obvious and sometimes it is subtle. Obvious examples might unfold when members of a particular race, religion, or ethnicity are not considered for jobs at museums about a particular race, religion, or ethnicity they are not part of. Age may be a factor unduly influencing job seekers, be an applicant younger or older than what a museum might desire.

Proving discrimination can be difficult. Moreover, a job seeker may prefer to avoid conflict that might jeopardize his or her reputation and thus interfere with employment elsewhere.

CONCLUSION

Generally speaking museum employment procedures and processes are fairly uniform in behavior, approach, and outcome. Jobs are advertised, applications are accepted, interviews take place, references and other information is requested and assessed, and someone is hired. Occasionally the time it takes to reach a conclusion is fast, as might be the case when hiring a pre-designated candidate, usually from within an organization. Occasionally it takes a long time to fill a position. Whether a museum job application is customary or odd, candidates are at the mercy of an employer. The more experience a person has with seeking employment, the more prepared she or he will be for each hiring situation. Always look at the big picture and how you fit in it. Museums are fascinating places to work in. Do not be overwhelmed by job prospects when starting your career. You are not alone; and though your colleagues may be your competition, they are also your support team.

NOTES

1. Maya Salam, "Brooklyn Museum Defends Its Hiring of a White Curator of African Art," *The New York Times*, April 6, 2016, https://www.nytimes.com/2018/04/06/arts/brooklyn-museum-african-arts.html.

2. Robin Pogrebin, "With New Urgency, Museums Cultivate Curators of Color, *The New York Times*, August 8, 2018, https://www.nytimes.com/2018/08/08/arts/design/museums-curators-diversity-employment.html.

Chapter Nine

The Future of Museum Professions

JOBS AND THE FUTURE OF MUSEUMS

The stature of museums has changed dramatically in the United States over the last fifty years. There are more of them. They are better known by the public. They enjoy extremely high levels of trust. They are admired for content and purpose. "Museum quality" denotes high praise, regardless of its application. The adulation museums enjoy will continue for a long time. This, of course, will have a positive impact on employment.

Going forward, most museum positions will exist as currently configured in identity and duty. These will continue to include director, curator, conservator, educator, guard, exhibit designer, rental coordinator, and fundraiser. The responsibilities for these and the other jobs outlined in chapter 2 will pretty much continue as described.

Of course, new skills must be learned as technology maintains an inexorable pace of change. This will unfold in how museums are physically run and how they meet their public programming mission. The IT front will have a special impact on exhibitions, education, marketing, and events.

The demographics of museum employees will alter to reflect the new demographics of America, but the need to work together in a productive, respectful, and timely manner will remain essential regardless of the mix of race, gender, ethnicity, religious beliefs or disbeliefs, education, wealth, etc. in the workplace.

A few new museum jobs will be created largely focused on audience development, expanding education options, and inter-institution collaborative ventures. There will be more temporary project-based, contractor, hourly, consulting, and seasonal jobs. This will benefit self-employed people who independently specialize in one of the many museum professions, and profession needs, listed in chapter 2. We see this already in the area of consulting curators for contemporary art exhibits. There are also contract collections managers who take on collection-specific projects with specific timeframes.

The basic work museums do now will change little. These odd institutions will still collect, preserve, study, and explain all manner of evidence of the human and natural universe. This is why mainstream current jobs will be rarely altered. Only the number and scope of them may be adjusted, reflecting a particular museum's capabilities and interests.

While museums will deal with responsibilities as they have in the past, their future development will emphasize several areas of already pressing concern. These will have unfolding employment consequences. The four most important priorities will be

- Collection Growth
- Increased Professionalism of the Field
- The Museum as Attraction
- The Survival of Individual Museums.

Collection Growth

Museum collections rarely shrink. They grow constantly. There are several reasons for this, but the cause is largely curatorial in origin. This will not stop. The idea of a museum ceasing to collect suggests a museum is dead. As a result of unbridled collecting, museums are awash with objects of all sorts. They are beginning to address the matter. The focus is on defining more disciplined acquisition criteria and improving storage. Sometimes a museum will decide to remove collections and thus deaccessioning occurs.

Museum employees that should make decisions regarding collection magnitude are directors, curators, and collection managers. When trustees are involved, hopefully their role will only be in an oversight position. The opinion and advice of conservators, maintenance staff, and educators will often be sought.

Potential museum job applicants in the professions cited above will be more successful job hunters if they have had successful experience dealing with full collection storage issues, creating new collection policies, and articulating what a museum collects, why, and how.

Increased Professionalism

The idea that museum employees are professionals practicing particular crafts, skills, or disciplines is well accepted today. This was not always the case. In the not too distant past, dilettantes and amateurs were often found doing what high skilled and experienced employees do now. The establishment of a museum field is the result of four developments.

- An obvious awareness from within museums that the various positions (as listed in chapter 2) actually call for training and ability.
- Increased support for the full range of museum jobs by professional organizations such as the American Alliance of Museums and the American Association for State and Local History.
- The creation of the museum accreditation program by the American Alliance of Museums, which requires certain program, staffing, financial, and operating standards to be met if a museum wants this designation.
- The establishment of graduate museum studies programs nationwide.

Requirements to meet certain standards and expectations have accompanied the increased professionalism of all museum jobs. This will continue. Regardless of the position, it will be incumbent upon the person in it to practice to the highest level of his or her commitment and abilities. Museum programming, and exhibitions in particular, have undergone remarkable changes in the past few decades. This will continue, and museum staff should be aware of what that means for jobs. They need to be supportive agents of this welcome advance. For instance, how exhibitions are presented has altered dramatically. Design standards are much higher than they were years ago. Content must be obviously relevant and of superior quality. A shift in population demographics has seen a change in what museums show in their galleries. For example, objects that were once of anthropological interest only and exhibited as ethnographic curiosities in natural history museums are today considered the fine art of indigenous and tribal peoples worldwide. They are now welcomed in art museums.

Given the often-transparent nature of museums, the public is aware of professional levels of institutional operations, even if they cannot pinpoint specific examples. This burgeoning public discernment will require museums to improve the overall quality of their missions. This can be done only by hiring employees who know how to do their jobs to the best of their abilities with the resources at hand.

The increased demand for qualified employees will see a rise in the number of graduate programs for museum studies. The quality and relevance of these programs needs to be understood as museum jobs become even more specific in their employment requirements. Also, how employers view individual programs will be of immense relevance to students.

Staffing museums is a far more rigorous and serious pursuit than it has ever been. Now, much is required of both prospective employers and prospective employees when it comes to hiring. Seeking work and finding good employees is highly competitive. That will continue. Furthermore, genera-tional changes will result in younger professionals entering and assuming leadership positions in the field. There are character profiles for various generations, and these need to be understood going forward.

The Museum as Attraction

Without question, the driving force that is having an impact on everything museums do centers on the desire to get more visitors. Some see museums as money-making places of entertainment, along the lines of profit-generating amusement parks, casinos, and sports stadia. Nothing could be further from real-ity, especially when looked at from inside these unique cultural establishments.

The museum as attraction is a phenomenon that museums themselves have helped create. The inordinate attendance emphasis arose in the late 1960s and accelerated rapidly in the 1970s. It resulted from organizing exhibitions with popularity in mind. The movement emerged especially from two major mu-seums: The National Gallery of Art in Washington, DC, and the Metropolitan Museum of Art in New York City. Large and well-received exhibitions re-sulted in crowded galleries; unprecedented publicity hype; museum directors who assumed an almost rock star status; and expectations that museums were now more than just quiet warehouses of dusty, musty old stuff.

The new emphasis on attendance fostered the idea that a museum must prove its worth through enhanced visitation numbers, and those numbers could support profits from earned income. With more people, a museum would make money from sales shops, food services, space rentals, reproduc-ing collections, and hosting tour groups. This was partly wishful thinking by trustees who fobbed off their fundraising duties onto staff, with the expec-tation that they would balance the budget. It also led to the idea of selling collections to make money for operating costs, debt payment, or capital im-provements—all of which is forbidden by museum profession ethics.

Fortunately, this metric-centric approach to museum management has not totally suffocated the real reason for museums. Collections are at the core. Public programming is essential. Scholarship continues albeit somewhat al-tered. Yet, numbers have an impact that has affected how museum jobs are defined and how they are configured on the organization chart.

Museum job seekers must be cognizant of a museum's visitation quotient when applying for a museum position. Annual budgets project these figures. What those figures are based on will tell candidates what is expected of staff, even if a position seems unrelated to desired profitable ventures. Unless some magic universal museum funding source is discovered, the pressure to be more self-sustaining will be intense going forward.

From an employment perspective, as museums work harder and harder to attract visitors, people with excellent marketing skills will be ever more sought after. Promoting museums to audiences of all sorts will become common practice. Evening social events of no or little relevance to exhibitions, collections, missions, etc. are now common practice in museums. The use of museums for social occasions of all sorts will proliferate.

The Survival of Individual Museums

As previously noted, museums are expensive to operate. Costs will continue to rise, largely because of improvements in professional expertise and public expectations. The age of the do-it-yourself museum is over. On the front line, visitors will no longer tolerate crummy looking and static exhibits, dirty facilities, lousy or absent retail operations, poorly presented programs, and disrespectful staff. Internally, the museum field requires well cared for collections, valued scholarship, and highly professional staff and governance bodies. All of this adds to annual budgets. To date we have seen few museums close. Despite all the operating challenges these unique institutions face, they stay afloat. Some even prosper. It is difficult to predict how long this state of affairs will endure.

Museums will accommodate change in several ways. Most will grow. A new museum age is starting to build upon the success of the current museum age. We will see existing museums expand and new ones created. While the most notable focus might appear to be on art museums, history and science museums will be keeping pace. This is good news for job seekers and those already in the field.

Every month it seems there is an announcement of a new museum being formed or an existing one expanding. Employees with experience in starting or growing museums will be in demand. Both accomplishments require specific skill sets, to happen successfully. Prospective applicants will need to be able to relocate, but the results can be enormously rewarding.

A change that will unfold in the future will be the loss of some museums entirely. Fortunately, they will be the exceptions. Mergers, acquisitions, transfers, consolidations, and reductions in scope and content will be more likely to occur as faltering museums seek to protect their collections and missions. We have seen this happen already with a few exceptional examples.

The Corcoran Gallery of Art in Washington, DC, dissolved in 2014, and its collections were given to area art museums while its art school was taken over by George Washington University.[1] In 2013, The Higgins Armory Museum in Worcester, MA, was absorbed by the Worcester Art Museum.[2] In 2017, the board of trustees of the Berkshire Museum in Pittsfield, MA, altered its focus and deaccessioned the major part of its American art collection.[3] In 2011, The Academy of Natural Sciences of Philadelphia, PA, was taken over by Drexel University in that city and is now the Academy of Natural Sciences of Drexel University.[4]

The evolving desire for museums to be ethnically, racially, economically, and gender diverse, as well as inclusive, accessible, and more broadly representative of the community they serve will escalate dramatically. Consequently, hiring will take on new ramifications. Prospective employees need to keep museum personnel and audience demographic realities in the back of their minds when looking for museum jobs. This will take time as people in good museum jobs are in no hurry to leave them. However, the Baby Boomer bubble is slowly deflating as that generation retires or dies. America's broadly diversifying population base will replace this coterie. In the museum field, the new arrivals will be better trained and scholastically prepared to lead these great institutions forward in a bold and more inclusive direction.

Museums will be more focused on increasing their endowments, if they have them, and creating ones, if they do not. These funds help secure operations. Even if the income is not enough to cover all annual expenses, every dollar helps. Endowments reduce fundraising pressure and thus allow museums more freedom to pursue their missions without relying on earned income. When times are tough financially, healthy endowments allow museums to navigate economic downturns. Finance and development positions within museums will be critical to their security, going forward. People with these skills can almost always be guaranteed jobs. Selecting trustees who recognize the value of endowments, and are willing to give or get funds to grow them, will be essential for governance planning.

"The future ain't what it used to be." —Yogi Berra

CONCLUSION

Museums are odd institutions. They are expected to change but stay the same. This contradiction is addressed daily as exhibitions are planned, acquisitions sought, research conducted, and public service roles defined. The considerable growth in the museum field over the past fifty years confirms their importance and value, be it for picayune local interests or for grand international concerns. Employment in these unique places will continue to expand.

Positions will become more defined insofar as qualifications, abilities, and experiences are concerned. An impressive academic résumé, when combined with relevant internships (paid or unpaid), and excellent references, will provide a critical competitive edge when seeking a first job. Once established in the museum field, developing a résumé of quantifiable accomplishments, knowledge, and experience will be the obvious norm. Museums are in the "show and tell" business. Therefore, the better a job candidate is at showing and telling, the better he or she will be in finding work. Selling yourself within the museum world is an acquired skill.

NOTES

1. Philip Kennicott, "The End of the Corcoran Gallery of Art," *Washington Post*, February 19, 2014, https://www.washingtonpost.com/entertainment/museums/the-end-of-the-corcoran-gallery-of-art/2014/02/19/accd8a38-99a3-11e3-b931-0204122c514b_story.html?utm_term=.cb2700bca94f.

2. Geoff Edgers, "Higgins Armory Museum to Close," *Boston Globe*, March 8, 2013, https://www.bostonglobe.com/arts/2013/03/08/higgins-armory-museum-close-arms-and-armor-worcester-art-museum/3Y4p45OpkfMrQxSGmlP3NP/story.html.

3. Jeff Jacoby, "The Berkshire Museum Saga Is Headed toward a Happy Ending," *Boston Globe*, April 18, 2018, https://www.bostonglobe.com/opinion/2018/04/18/the-berkshire-museum-saga-headed-toward-happy-ending/v2ZBYbRbCfhs4XjEQsvKWL/story.html.

4. "The Academy of Natural Sciences and Drexel University Announce a Historic Affiliation," Academy of Natural Sciences of Drexel University, accessed September 2, 2018, http://ansp.org/about/drexel-affiliation/.

Index

19–20; applying for, 61–69; collection management and registration staff, 16–17; conservator, 23–24, *23;* curator, 14–16, *15;* director, 32–34; earned income staff, 26–27, *26;* educator, 10–11, *12;* exhibition staff, 11–14, *13;* financial staff, 31–32; full-time, 57–59; fundraiser, 21–23; future of, 113–119; information technology staff, 17–18, *17;* job ad, 59–60; job listings, 55–60; maintenance staff, 29, *30,* 31; marketing/public relations/media staff, 24–26, *25;* part-time, 59; other jobs, 34; security staff, 27–29, *28;* visitor services staff, 20–21

MuseumJobsOnline.com, 56

museum life, 3–7

museum life cycles, 42–46; changing museums, 45; failing museums, 45–46; long-established museums, 42–43; museums in formation, 44; new museums, 44–45

museum location, 51–52

Museum Management Consultants, Inc., 57, 105

Museum Market, 56

Museum of the City of New York, curatorial department, *15*

museum ownership, 46–61; academic museums, 49–50; company museums, 49; government-owned museums, 47–48; individually owned museums, 46–47; museum facilities owned by a larger entity, 50–51; private nonprofit charities, 47

museums: as attraction, 116–117; attributes, xii–xiv; collections, 16–17; definition of, 2; disciplines, 38; future of and jobs, 113–118; history of, 1–2; job-seeking, 3–7; life cycles, 42–46; location of, 51–52; ownership, 46–51; research about,

52–54; selecting, 37–54; size and physical premises, 39–42; survival of, 117–118; tax-exempt status, 10; world of, 2–3; and you, 1–7

museum size, 39–41; large museums, 40; medium-sized museums, 40; small museums, 40–41

museum-specific websites, 56

museum world, 2–3

new jobs. *See* full-time museum jobs

New York Foundation for the Arts, 56

online employment sources, 55–57

Opportunity Resources, Inc., 105

part-time museum jobs, 59

personal demographics. *See* demographics

physical premises, 41–42

private nonprofit charities, 47

professionalism, increase of, 114–116

public relations staff, 6

questions. *See* interview questions

reconfigured jobs. *See* full-time museum jobs

references, 67

request to apply for a job. *See* invitation to apply for a job

researching museums, 52–54

résumés, 15, 63–66; one-page example, 65

Russell Reynolds Associates, 57, 105

salaries, low, 6

The Scream, security for, *28*

search firms, 56–57, 105–106

secretary. *See* administrative assistant

security staff, 27–29, *28*

Seton Hall University MA Program in Museum Professions, field trip, *13*

seven Ps, 33

About the Author

Steven Miller has been in the museum field nearly fifty years. During that time, he has served as a trustee, director, curator, consultant, writer, educator, and lecturer as well as media commentator on various topics relating to museum philosophy and operations. He is affiliated with the Museum Accreditation Program of the American Alliance of Museums. For sixteen years he was an adjunct professor teaching several courses with the Seton Hall University MA Program in Museum Professions. He is the author of *The Anatomy of a Museum: An Insider's Text* (2018) and *Deaccessioning Today: Theory and Practice (*2018*)*. He holds a BA in sculpture from Bard College and an International Graduate Certificate from ICCROM (International Centre for the Study of the Preservation and Restoration of Cultural Property, Rome, Italy). He lives with his wife, Jane, in Doylestown, PA. They have two children, one of whom is also in the museum field.